MODELLING THE CITY

— CROSS-CULTURAL PERSPECTIVES —

D1702531

Colloquium Geographicum

ISSN 0588 - 3253

Herausgegeben von W.Lauer,K.-A.Boesler,G.Aymans und E.Ehlers

Schriftleitung: H. - J. Ruckert

Band 22

MODELLING THE CITY
— CROSS-CULTURAL PERSPECTIVES —

Vorträge gehalten aus Anlaß der Verleihung der Ehrendoktorwürde der
Mathematisch—Naturwissenschaftlichen Fakultät der
Rheinischen Friedrich—Wilhelms—Universität Bonn an
Professor Chauncy D. Harris. Ph. D., D. Litt., Drs. h. c., Chicago

Herausgegeben

von

ECKART EHLERS

1992

In Kommission bei
FERD. DÜMMLERS VERLAG · BONN
—Dümmlerbuch 7422 —

Z - 143

(Neuw.: PC-II)

MODELLING THE CITY
— CROSS-CULTURAL PERSPECTIVES —

Herausgegeben von
Eckart Ehlers

Mit 39 Figuren, 4 Tabellen und einem Foto

Inv.-Nr. A 22 602

Mit Beiträgen von

Jürgen Bähr, Eckart Ehlers, Chauncy D. Harris,
Burkhard Hofmeister, Elisabeth Lichtenberger,
Walther Manshard, Günter Mertins,
Wolfgang Taubmann, Herbert Wilhelmy

Geographisches Institut
der Universität Kiel
ausgesonderte Dublette

Geographisches Institut
der Universität Kiel
Neue Universität

In Kommission bei

FERD. DÜMMLERS VERLAG · BONN

Dümmlerbuch 7422

Alle Rechte vorbehalten

ISBN 3-427-**7422**1—0

© 1992 **Ferd. Dümmlers Verlag, 5300 Bonn 1**

Herstellung: Druckerei Plump, 5342 Rheinbreitbach

VORWORT

Der vorliegende Band des Colloqium Geographicum vereint die Vorträge, die im Rahmen eines Festkolloquiums aus Anlaß der Verleihung der Ehrendoktorwürde der Mathematisch-Naturwissenschaftlichen Fakultät der Rheinischen Friedrich-Wilhelms-Universität an Professor Dr. Drs. h.c. mult. Chauncy D. Harris (Chicago) am 4. Februar 1991in Bonn gehalten wurden.

Der Text der Verleihungsurkunde macht deutlich, daß die Ehrung nicht nur Dank und Anerkennung der Bonner Geographen, sondern der deutschen Geographie schlechthin ausdrückt. Die Ehrendoktorwürde wurde an Professor Harris verliehen

- aufgrund seiner methodisch richtungsweisenden Arbeiten zur Stadtgeographie, in denen er zum Mitbegründer funktionaler Betrachtungsweise und raumwissenschaftlicher Modellbildung wurde;
- aufgrund seiner in der internationalen Geographie der Nachkriegszeit unermüdlichen Bemühungen um wissenschaftliche Kooperation und Verständigung über Ideologie- und Ländergrenzen hinweg;
- aufgrund seiner herausragenden Verdienste um die Wiederaufnahme der Geographie der Bundesrepublik Deutschland in die Internationale Geographische Union nach dem Zweiten Weltkrieg.

Das Thema des Festkolloqiums entsprach einem Wunsch und Vorschlag des Jubilars. Möge das Bändchen nicht nur ihm, sondern auch der internationalen Fachwelt Einblick in einen seit langem in der deutschen Geographie gepflegten Zweig stadtgeographischer Forschung geben.

Bonn, im Juli 1991   Eckart Ehlers

Chauncy D. Harris bei seinem Vortrag in Bonn
am 4.2.1991

INHALT

7

LAUDATIO CHAUNCY D. HARRIS

Herbert Wilhelmy

Das im Jahre 1903 begründete Department of Geography an der Universität Chicago war das erste Geographische Institut einer amerikanischen Universität, aus dem graduierte Geographen hervorgegangen sind.[1] Die Reihe der dort tätig gewesenen akademischen Lehrer beginnt mit Rollin S. Salisbury und J. Paul Goode. Salisbury war zeitweise Student bei Hettner in Heidelberg gewesen, Goode hatte in Ermanglung einer Promotionsmöglichkeit im Fach Geographie den wirtschaftswissenschaftlichen Doktorgrad an der Universität von Pennsylvania erworben. Das bis 1919 von Salisbury geleitete Department nahm einen beachtlichen Aufschwung und mehrte sein Ansehen in den 20er Jahren durch die Berufung einer Anzahl namhafter Gastprofessoren aus Europa, wie Sten de Geer, Helge Nelson, Raoul Blanchard und Albrecht Penck. Die Institutsdirektoren der Jahre 1919 bis 1956 waren Harlan H. Barrows (1919–1942), Charles C. Colby (1942–1949) und Robert S. Platt (1949–1956). Bis in die 40er Jahre bestand der Lehrkörper des Instituts nur jeweils aus einem Professor und mehreren Instruktoren. 1943 vergrößerte er sich um einen Assistant Professor: Chauncy D. Harris. Nachdem seit 1929 in Chicago stets nur Instruktorenstellen geschaffen und besetzt worden waren, war diese Assistenzprofessur die erste gehobene Stelle, die das Department erhielt.

Chauncy D. Harris, Jahrgang 1914, stammt aus Logan im Mormonenstaat Utah. In Salt Lake City studierte er an der Brigham Young University, ging dann nach Erwerb des Bakkalaureats (1933) nach Chicago und von dort mit einem Rhodes-Stipendium nach Oxford. 1936/37 setzte er seine Studien an der London School of Economics fort und kehrte nach den üblichen Abschlußexamen 1939 in die Staaten zurück. An der Indiana University begann er seine akademische Lehrtätigkeit als Instructor in Geography, wurde 1940 in Chicago mit einer Arbeit „Salt Lake City, A Regional Capital" zum Ph. D. promoviert und bereits im folgenden Jahr auf eine Assistenzprofessur an die Universität in Nebraska berufen. Dort blieb er bis zu seinem Wechsel in gleicher Position an die Universität von Chicago, die für mehr als 40 Jahre, von 1943 bis zu seiner Emeritierung im Jahre 1984 (und darüber hinaus bis zum heutigen Tage) seine akademische Wirkungsstätte werden sollte. Die weiteren Stationen seiner Karriere folgen dicht aufeinander: 1946 Associate Professor, 1947 o. Professor, 1969 Samuel N. Harper Professor und ab 1973 Samuel N. Harper Distinguished Service Professor. Harris war Institutsdirektor, Dekan, rechte Hand des Universitätspräsidenten und in vielen anderen Funktionen an seiner Hochschule tätig. Von seinem Engagement in nationalen und internationalen Fachorganisationen wird noch die Rede sein.

In seinem wissenschaftlichen Werdegang haben den jungen Chauncy Harris Männer wie Wellington D. Jones und Robert S. Platt nachhaltig beeinflußt. Jones machte ihn mit den Methoden der Auswertung statistischer Erhebungen vertraut, Platt führte ihn in die geographische Feldarbeit ein. Harris erkannte frühzeitig die vielfältigen Möglichkeiten, die sich aus der Kombination detaillierter Forschung im Gelände mit statistischer Analyse ergaben. Alle seine späteren Arbeiten bezeugen dies. In die Probleme der kartographischen Darstellung führte ihn J. Paul Goode ein, der durch seine eigenartig gelappten mehrpoligen, flächentreuen Netzentwürfe bekannt geworden ist. Griffith Taylor, der ebenfalls in Chicago lehrte und wie Platt auf Exkursionen und in mehrtägigen oder auch wochenlangen Geländepraktika die jungen Studenten für geographische Fragestellungen und Forschungsarbeit zu begeistern verstand, wurde Harris erstmalig auf einen deutschen Geographen aufmerksam gemacht, der in den 20er Jahren ergebnisreiche Forschungsreisen in den südamerikanischen Anden durchgeführt hatte: Carl Troll. Zu ihm sollten sich später enge fachliche und freundschaftliche Beziehungen entwickeln. Die Möglichkeit, in Chicago Vorlesungen John A. Morrisons über die Sowjetunion zu hören, hat Harris, wie er zu seinem Bedauern später bekundet, nicht genutzt – sein Interesse an der Sowjetunion erwachte erst nach Abschluß der Studienzeit.

Ein entscheidender Anstoß für seine künftige geographische Lebensarbeit entstammt jedoch noch den Studentenjahren, und zwar vor allem den Diskussionen mit seinem Kommilitonen Edward L. Ullmann. Er lenkte Chauncy Harris' Blick auf die Stadt- und Verkehrsgeographie, und die Stadtgeographie ist denn auch zum tragenden Thema seines wissenschaftlichen Schaffens geworden.

Den Auftakt dazu stellte seine 1940 der Universität von Chicago vorgelegte Dissertation dar: „Salt Lake City, A Regional Capital"[2]. Die Hauptergebnisse dieser nur schwer zugänglichen Arbeit veröffentlichte er 1941 in einem Aufsatz in der Zeitschrift Economic Geography unter dem bezeichnenden Titel „Location of Salt Lake City"[3]. Denn es ging Harrris darum zu zeigen, welcher Art die physischgeographischen und anthropogeographischen Voraussetzungen für die Entwicklung dieser größten Stadt zwischen Denver und der pazifischen Küste sind. Es sind dies der Wasserreichtum der am Fuß der gut beregneten Wasatch Mts. inmitten der wüstenhaften Umwelt des Großen Beckens gelegenen Bewässerungsoase, die fruchtbaren Böden der Seeterrassen des pleistozänen Lake Bonneville, die für landwirtschaftliche Kulturen günstigen sonstigen klimatischen Bedingungen, der relativ leichte Übergang über die Wasatch Mts. in ostwestlicher Richtung, dem die große Westwanderung und die erste transkontinentale Eisenbahn folgten. Hinzu kam der Reichtum an Bodenschätzen und nicht zuletzt der Wille der Mormonen-Pioniere, die die Erkenntnisse früher Forschungsreisender benutzten und in einer klugen Entscheidung 1847 den heutigen Platz für ihre Ansiedlung in selbst gewählter, freilich nicht lange andauernder Einsamkeit bestimmten.

Von der großen Stadtmonographie, dem eingehend analysierten Spezialfall im Mormonenland, führte der Weg zur Darlegung allgemeingültiger stadtgeographischer Erkenntnisse. 1943 und 1945 veröffentlichte Harris die beiden Aufsätze

10

„A Functional Classification of Cities in the United States"[4] und zusammen mit dem alten Freund Edward L. Ullmann „The Nature of Cities"[5]. Die eine Arbeit wurde viermal in Sammelwerken, die andere sogar zehnmal wieder abgedruckt. Peter Schöller hat beide auch in den von ihm herausgegebenen Band „Allgemeine Stadtgeographie" der Wissenschaftlichen Buchgemeinschaft übernommen. Ihre Bedeutung beruht darauf, daß Harris über die längst geläufigen Begriffe Industrie-, Handels-, Bergbau-, Verwaltungs-, Universitätsstadt usw. exakte Kriterien für die jeweilige Zuordnung eines städtischen Gemeinwesens herausarbeitet. In der Regel erfüllt jede Stadt mit mehr als 25.000 Einwohnern verschiedene Funktionen. Die nähere Kennzeichnung einer Stadt nur nach äußeren Merkmalen kann daher fehlerhaft sein. Harris sieht in statistischen Daten eine vertrauenswürdigere Basis und ermittelt über die Beschäftigtenzahlen anhand empirisch gewonnener Grenz- und Schwellenwerte die Rangordnung der Funktionen. Sein am Beispiel der US-amerikanischen Städte erprobtes Verfahren ist in der Folgezeit in vielen anderen Ländern angewendet worden.

Der zweite Aufsatz über die Natur der Städte untersucht die Abhängigkeit der jeweils herausragenden Strukturelemente von der Lage der betreffenden Stadt unter den Gesichtspunkten ihrer Zentralität und Verkehrssituation. Es werden in Anlehnung an Christaller Modelle der theoretischen Ordnung zentraler Plätze verschiedenen Ranges, sodann auf Grund eigener Überlegungen solche verkehrsabhängiger oder speziell standortbedingter Siedlungen entworfen. Aus der Kombination dieser drei Modelle ergibt sich ein weitgehend der Wirklichkeit entsprechendes Bild der räumlichen Verteilung von Städten unterschiedlicher Funktionalität. Umgekehrt lassen sich real existierende, kartographisch fixierte Verteilungsbilder in die drei genannten Ordnungsmuster auflösen. Dieses Verfahren ermöglicht tiefere Einsichten in das zu analysierende Raumgefüge und dessen Genese. Es läßt sich im Prinzip auch individuell auf jede zu untersuchende Stadt anwenden und erlaubt deren Gliederung in ringförmig angeordnete funktionale Zonen, Sektoren oder Kerne mit auffälliger Konzentration bestimmter struktureller Erscheinungen. Harris' Grundschema hat in der stadtgeographischen Forschung weitergewirkt, z.B. in der Erarbeitung eines Idealschemas für die lateinamerikanische Stadt durch Bähr, Mertins, Borsdorf und Gormsen.

Im gleichen Jahr 1945, als die Arbeit „The Nature of Cities" erschien, veröffentlichte Harris seinen Aufsatz „The Cities of the Soviet Union".[6] Er ist aus zwei Gründen für die Würdigung von Harris' Lebensarbeit wichtig: Einmal dokumentiert der Verfasser in dieser Studie die praktische Anwendung seiner Methode, indem er ein klares Bild des Wachstums, der Funktion und der Verteilung der städtischen Zentren in einem außeramerikanischen großen Lande zeichnet, zum anderen, daß es sich dabei um die Sowjetunion handelt, der er fortan einen Großteil seines wissenschaftlichen Werkes gewidmet hat. Neben den Vereinigten Staaten ist seit Kriegsende die Sowjetunion zum regionalen Schwerpunkt seiner stadtgeographischen Forschungen geworden. Das Resultat seines jahrzehntelangen Mühens, wozu auch die Erlernung der russischen Sprache, die Beschaffung und

11

Verarbeitung einer schwer zugänglichen, umfangreichen Literatur gehörten, ist sein 1970 in erster und schon 1972 in zweiter Auflage erschienenes Werk „Cities of the Soviet Union"[7]. Aber dies ist keineswegs eine reine Literaturarbeit. Im Rahmen eines akademischen Austauschprogramms zwischen dem American Council of Learned Studies und der sowjetischen Akademie der Wissenschaften konnte sich Harris 1963, nachdem er ein paar Jahre zuvor einer Einladung der Sowjetischen Geographischen Gesellschaft gefolgt war, erneut mehrere Monate in der Sowjetunion aufhalten, dort Fall- und Literaturstudien betreiben und sich ein umfangreiches statistisches Material erschließen. Viele sowjetische Kollegen unterstützten den renommierten Wissenschaftler, der damals bereits Vizepräsident der Internationalen Geographischen Union war und der sich in der Folgezeit trotz aller politischen Hindernisse große Verdienste um einen amerikanisch-sowjetischen Wissenschaftleraustausch erworben hat. Mehr als 20 Aufsätze über osteuropäische Themen und die Übersetzungen dreier wichtiger Sammelwerke sowjetischer Geographen hat Harris veröffentlicht, darunter die von Balzak u.a. herausgegebene Wirtschaftsgeographie der UdSSR[8] und die Soviet Geography, in der 56 Symposiumsbeiträge führender Geographen der Union vereinigt sind.[9]

Im letzten Jahrzehnt hat Harris seine stadtgeographischen Studien auch auf Japan ausgedehnt, wo er auf Einladung der Japanischen Gesellschaft zur Förderung der Wissenschaft einen intensiv genutzten Forschungsaufenthalt verbrachte.[10][11] Daraus ergab sich ein fruchtbarer Gedankenaustausch mit Peter Schöller, dessen allzu früher Tod ihn sehr berührte und dessen Leistung er in seinem Nachruf in der Zeitschrift Urban Geography würdigte.[12]

Als Chauncy Harris die Literatur für sein russisches Städtebuch sichtete, beschränkte er sich nicht auf die Sammlung des einschlägigen stadtgeographischen Schrifttums. Er erfaßte auch eine Fülle wichtiger in- und ausländischer Bibliophien zur Landeskunde der Sowjetunion und publizierte ein daraus erwachsenes Kompendium von 2.600 Titeln in detaillierter sachlicher und regionaler Ordnung.[13] Dieses Werk läßt einen weiteren Wesenszug von Harris erkennen: die Liebe zur bibliographischen Arbeit, zur Überschaubarmachung des geographischen und geographisch relevanten vielschichtigen Schrifttums. Er hatte schon seit 1950 begonnen, zusammen mit Jerome D. Fellman Zusammenstellungen weltweit erscheinender geographischer Zeitschriften und Schriftenreihen zu veröffentlichen, die, immer wieder ergänzt, im Abstand weniger Jahre erschienen und als „International List of Geographical Series" zu einer unentbehrlichen Informationsquelle geworden sind.[14] Dazu kam im Laufe der Jahre eine Reihe von allgemein-geographischen Bibliographien für Bibliotheks- und Studienzwecke, teils in regionaler Spezialisierung. Der stattliche Band der Unions-Bibliographie, dem selbst die Russen bis heute kein entsprechendes Werk an die Seite zu stellen haben, legte Harris 1975 vor, sozusagen als persönliche Festgabe für den 1976 in Moskau veranstalteten 23. Internationalen Geographen-Kongreß oder – wenn man so will – als Festgabe des langjährigen Generalsekretärs und Schatzmeisters der IGU.

Damit sind wir bei der Würdigung des Wirkens von Chauncy Harris in den nationalen und internationalen Organisationen unseres Faches angelangt. Schon 1957/58 war er Präsident der Association of American Geographers, 1969–74 Vizepräsident der American Geographical Society. 1956 bis 1964 wurde er als Vizepräsident in den Vorstand der Internationalen Geographischen Union gewählt, und acht Jahre lang, von 1968–76, bekleidete er das arbeitsreiche Amt eines Generalsekretärs und Schatzmeisters der Union, der auch für das pünktliche Erscheinen der IGU-Informationen zu sorgen hatte. Seine hervorragende Beherrschung mehrerer Sprachen kam ihm nicht nur in seiner wissenschaftlichen Arbeit zustatten – sie machte ihn auch zu einem schlagfertigen Diskussionspartner und versierten Verhandlungsleiter. An sämtlichen internationalen Kongressen zwischen 1949 und 1984 – von Lissabon über Washington, Rio de Janeiro, Stockholm, London, New Delhi, Montreal, Moskau, Tokio und Paris – hat er teilgenommen. Wer ihm dort amtlich oder privat begegnet ist, wird den Menschen Chauncy Harris nicht vergessen: diesen immer Heiterkeit und Ruhe ausstrahlenden Mann, der, obwohl ständig in Anspruch genommen, nie gehetzt wirkt und immer Zeit für ein freundschaftliches Gespräch hat. So – und dieses persönliche Wort sei mir gestattet – habe ich ihn erlebt, in Rio, New Delhi und Montreal. Aber meine Bekanntschaft mit ihm geht viel weiter zurück. Anfang der 50er Jahre hielt ich einen Vortrag in Frankfurt, und im Gästezimmer des dortigen Geographischen Instituts blickte mich auf einem Scherenschnitt Chauncy Harris an. Ich lernte ihn also zunächst einmal im Bilde kennen. 1950/51 hatte er nämlich an der Johann Wolfgang v. Goethe Universität auf Einladung Herbert Lehmanns eine Gastprofessur inne, und die Erinnerung an jenen frühen Aufenthalt in Nachkriegsdeutschland hielt jener Scherenschnitt fest. Harris hat sich übrigens damals mit dem deutschen Flüchtlingsproblem beschäftigt und darüber 1953 zusammen mit Gabriele Wülker in der Economic Geography berichtet.[15] Persönlich begegnet sind wir uns dann erstmalig 1956 auf dem Kongreß in Rio de Janeiro, an dem wir beide in offizieller EIgenschaft teilnahmen: er als Vizepräsident der IGU, ich als Leiter der deutschen Geographen-Delegation. 1959, auf dem Wege zur Wahrnehmung einer Gastprofessur in Berkeley, besuchte ich ihn in Chicago, und er vermittelte meiner Frau und mir einen umfassenden Eindruck dieser Stadt. 1966 sahen wir uns in Mexiko. Als sich dort seine Frau Edith am Stachel einer Agave erheblich verletzte, konnte ich ihr erste Hilfe leisten.

Doch zurück zu dem Mann, dem diese Feier gilt. Die Zahl der Ehrungen, die Chauncy Harris zuteil geworden sind, läßt sich kaum überschauen. Er ist Ehrendoktor der Katholischen Universität von Chile und der Indiana University, Ehrenmitglied von zehn traditionsreichen Geographischen Gesellschaften, darunter der Gesellschaft für Erdkunde zu Berlin, der Royal Geographical Society in London und der Società Geografica Italiana. Die Berliner Gesellschaft verlieh ihm 1978 die Goldene Alexander v. Humboldt-Medaille, die Royal Society die Victoria-Medaille. Viele nationale und internationale Gremien zählten und zählen ihn zu ihrem Mitglied. Zwei Festschriften wurden ihm gewidmet: 1984 anläßlich seiner Emeritierung eine Sammlung von 13 Essays zur Geographie der Sowjetunion[16] und 1986 der noch erheblich umfangreichere Band zum anderen wissenschaftlichen Schwerpunkt "World Patterns of Modern Urban Change".[17] Ich beschließe diese Laudatio und meine, daß sich das Gesagte zu einem klaren Bild zusammenfügt: Chauncy Harris ist eine Forscherpersönlichkeit von internationalem Rang. Wir Geographen dürfen stolz darauf sein, ihn zu den Unseren zu zählen.

ZITIERTE ARBEITEN VON CHAUNCY D. HARRIS

[1] "Geography at Chicago in the 1930s and 1940s", *Annals of the Association of American Geographers*, Vol. 69, No. 1 (March 1979), pp. 21−32.

[2] "Salt Lake City, A Regional Capital." Ph. D. Dissertation, Department of Geography, University of Chicago, 1940 (Chicago: University of Chicago Libraries, 1940). 206 pp. Planographed.

[3] "Location of Salt Lake City," *Economic Geography*, Vol. 17, No. 2 (April 1941), pp. 204−212.
Reprinted in: *Bobbs-Merrill Reprint Series in Geography*, G−83

[4] "A Functional Classification of Cities in the United States," *Geographical Review*, Vol. 33, No. 1 (January, 1943), pp. 86−99.
Reprinted in: *Readings in Urban Geography*, editet by HAROLD M. MAYER and CLYDE F. KOHN. (Chicago: University of Chicago Press, 1959), pp. 129−138.
Reprinted in *The Sociology of Urban Life: A Text book with Readings*, by T. LYNN SMITH and C. A. MCMAHAN (New York: Dryden Press, 1951), pp. 84−97.
Translated into Russian as "Funktsional'naia klassifikatsiia gorodov S.Sh.A.", in *Geografiia Gorodov*. Moskva, "Progress," 1965, pp. 121−134.
Reprinted in: *Allgemeine Stadtgeographie*, herausgegeben von PETER SCHÖLLER (Darmstadt: Wissenschaftliche Buchgesellschaft, 1969), pp. 289−309.

[5] "The Nature of Cities," *Annals of the American Academy of Political and Social Science*, Vol. 242 (November, 1945), pp. 7−17 (with EDWARD L. ULLMAN).
Reprinted in:
Reader in Urban Sociology, edited by PAUL K. HATT and ALBERT J. REISS, Jr. (Glencoe, Illinois: The Free Press, 1951), pp. 222−232.
Outside Readings in Geography, edited by FRED E. DOHRS, LAWRENCE M. SOMERS, and DONALD D. PETTERSON (New York: Thomas Y. Crowell, 1955) pp. 659−670.
Cities and Society: The Revised Reader in Urban Sociology (Glencoe, Illinois: The Free Press, 1957), pp. 237−247. (PAUL K. HATT and ALBERT J. REISS, Jr.).
Readings in Urban Geography, editet by HAROLD M. MAYER and CLYDE F. KOHN, (Chicago: University of Chicago Press, 1959), pp. 277−286.
Bobbs-Merrill Reprint Series in Geography G−85 (Indianapolis: Bobbs-Merrill, 1968)
Allgemeine Stadtgeographie, edited by PETER SCHÖLLER (Darmstadt: Wissenschaftliche Buchgesellschaft, 1969), pp. 220−237.
A Geography of Urban Places, edited by ROBERT G. PUTNAM, FRANK J. TAYLOR, and PHILIP G. KETTLE (Toronto and London: Methuen, 1970), pp. 91−101.

The Sociology of the City, edited by Sandor Halebsky (New York: Charles Scribner's Sons, 1973), pp. 102—115.

Comparative Urban Structure: Studies in the Ecology of Cities, edited by Kent P. Schwirian (Lexington, Mass.: D. C. Heath, 1974), pp. 217—226.

Translated into Russian as "Sushchnost' Gorodov," in *Geografiia Gorodov,* Translated by V. M. Gokhman, edited by V. V. Pokshisevskii (Moskva: Izdatel'stvo "Progress," 1965), pp. 255—268.

6) "The Cities of the Soviet Union," *Geographical Review,* Vol. 35, No. 1 (January, 1945), pp. 107—121.

Reprinted in part as: "Las Cuidades de la Unión Soviética," *Revista Geográfica Americana,* Vol. 23, No. 140 (May, 1945), pp. 292—296.

7) *"Cities of the Soviet Union: Studies in Their Functions, Size, Density, and Growth".* "Association of American Geographers, Monograph No. 5," (Chicago: Rand McNally and Co., 1970), xxviii plus 484 pp. (Second printing, Washington: Association of American Geographers, 1972).

8) *"Economic Geography of the U.S.S.R. ",* edited by S. S. Balzak, V. F. Vasyutin, and Ya. G. Feigin. American edition edited by Chauncy D. Harris "Russian Translation Project, American Council of Learned Societies." (New York Macmillan, 1949). 620 pp.

9) *Soviet Geography: Accomplishments and Tasks.* A Symposium of 50 chapters, contributed by 56 leading Soviet geographers and edited by a committee of the Geographic Society of the U.S.S.R., Academy of Siences of the U.S.S.R., I. P. Gerasimov, chairman. English edition edited by Chauncy D. Harris, "American Geographical Society, Occasional Publication No. 1," (New York: American Geographical Society, 1962). 409 pp.

10) "The Urban and Industrial Transformation of Japan" *Geographical Review,* vol. 72, no. 1 (January, 1982), pp. 50—89.

11) "Urban Geography in Japan: A Survey of Recent Literature," *Urban Geography,* vol. 3, no. 1 (January-March, 1982), pp. 1—21 (with Richard Louis Edmonds).

12) „Peter Schöller, 1923—1988," *Urban Geography,* vol. 9, no. 4 (July—August, 1988) p. 393—396.

13) *Guide to Geographical Bibliographies and Reference Works in Russian or on the Soviet Union.* University of Chicago, Department of Geography, Research Paper No. 164. 1975. xviii plus 478 pp.

14) *International List of Geographical Serials.* 3rd. ed., "University of Chicago, Department of Geography Research Paper No. 193," 1980. 457 pp. (with Jerome D. Fellmann).

15) "The Refugee Problem of Germany," *Economic Geography,* Vol. 29, No. 1 (January, 1953), pp. 10—25, (with Gabriele Wülker).

16) *Geographical Studies on the Soviet Union.* Essays in Honor of Chauncy D. Harris. George J. Demko and Roland J. Fuchs, editors. Chicago: University of Chicago, Department of Geography, Research Paper no. 211, 1984. 294 pp.

17) *World Patterns of Modern Urban Change.* Essays in Honor of Chauncy D. Harris. Michael P. Conzen, editor. Chicago: University of Chicago, Department of Geography, Research Paper no. 217—218. 1986. 479 pp.

CHAUNCY D. HARRIS
SELECTED BIBLIOGRAPHY
1940–1991

This Bibliography is in four sections:
A. Separate volumes written, compiled, or edited
B. Geographical articles, chapters in books, or small booklets
C. Addresses and general articles
D. Memorials and appreciations

A. Separate volumes written, compiled, or edited

1. Salt Lake City: A Regional Capital. Ph. D. Dissertation, Department of Geography, University of Chicago, 1940. Chicago: Private edition distributed by the University of Chicago Libraries, 1940. 206 p. Planographed.
2. Economic Geography of the USSR, edited by S. S. BALZAK, V. F. VASYUTIN, and YA. G. FEIGIN. American edition edited by CHAUNCY D. HARRIS. Translated from Russian by ROBERT M. HANKIN and OLGA ADLER TITELBAUM. New York: Macmillan, 1949. 620 p. "American Council of Learned Society. Russian Translation Project."
3. Soviet Geography: Accomplishments and Tasks. A Symposium of 50 chapters, contributed by 56 leading Soviet geographers and edited by a committee of the Geographic Society of the USSR, Academy of Sciences of the USSR. I. P. GERASIMOV, chairman. English edition edited by CHAUNCY D. HARRIS. Translated from Russian by LAWRENCE ECKER. New York: American Geographical Society, 1962. 409 p. "American Geographical Society. Occasional Publication No. 1."
4. Cities of the Soviet Union: Studies in Their Functions, Size. Density, and Growth. Chicago: Rand McNally and Co., 1970. 484 p. 2nd printing, Washington, D.C: Association of American Geographers, 1972. "Association of American Geographers. Monograph No. 5."
5. Population of Cities of the Soviet Union, 1897, 1926, 1939, 1959, and 1967: Tables, Maps, and Gazetteer. New York: American Geographical Society, 1970, 138 p. Special issue of Soviet Geography: Review and Translation, vol. 11, no. 5 (May, 1970), p. 307–444.
6. Guide to Geographical Bibliographies and Reference Works in Russian or on the Soviet Union. Chicago: University of Chicago, Department of Geography, Research Paper No. 164. 1975. 478 p.
7. Bibliography of Geography: Part I. Introduction to General Aids. Chicago: University of Chicago, Department of Geography, Research Paper No. 179. 1976. 276 p.
8. International List of Geographical Serials. 3rd ed. Chicago: University of Chicago, Department of Geography, Research Paper No. 193. 1980. 457 p. (with JEROME D. FELLMANN). (1st ed., 1960. 194 p., 2nd ed., 1971. 267 p. Predecessor titles: A Comprehensive Checklist of Serials of Geographic Value, Part. I, Geographic Serials Proper, 1949. 100 p. A Union List of Geographical Serials, 2nd ed., 1950. 124 p.
9. Annotated World List of Selected Current Geographical Serials. 4th ed. Chicago: University of Chicago, Department of Geography, Research Paper No. 194, 1980. 165 p. (1st ed. 1960. 14 p., 2nd ed. 1964. 30 p., 3rd ed. 1971. 77 p.) Title varies.

10. Bibliography of Geography, Part 2, Regional. Volume 1, The United States of America. Chicago: University of Chicago, Department of Geography, Research Paper No. 206. 1984. 178 p.

11. A Geographical Bibliography for American Libraries. CHAUNCY D. HARRIS editor-in-chief. A Joint Project of the Association of American Geographers and the National Geographic Society. Washington, D.C.: Association of American Geographers, 1985. 437 p.

12. Directory of Soviet Geographers 1946–1987. Compiled by THEODORE SHABAD. Edited and Supplemented by CHAUNCY D. HARRIS. Silver Spring, MD: V. H. Winston and Sons, 1988. 274 p. Also as special double issue of Soviet Geography, vol. 29, nos. 2–3 (February-March 1988), p. 95–366.

B. Geographical articles, chapters in books, or small booklets

1. "Electricity Generation in London, England," Geographical Review, vol. 31, no. 1 (January, 1941), p. 127–134.

2. "Location of Salt Lake City," Economic Geography, vol. 17, no. 2 (April, 1941), p. 204–212.
   Reprinted in Bobbs-Merrill Reprint Series in Geography, G-83. Indianapolis, IN: Bobbs-Merrill, 1968.

3. "Ipswich, England," Economic Geography, vol. 18, no. 1 (January, 1942), p. 1–12.

4. "Growth of Larger Cities in the United States 1930–1940," Journal of Geography, vol. 41, no. 8 (November, 1942), p. 313–318.

5. "The Metropolitan Districts in 1940," Journal of Geography, vol. 41, no. 9 (December, 1942), p. 340–343.

6. "A Functional Classification of Cities in the United States," Geographical Review, vol. 33, no. 1 (January, 1943), p. 86–99.
   Reprinted in Readings in Urban Geography, edited by HAROLD M. MAYER and CLYDE F. KOHN. Chicago: University of Chicago Press, 1959, p. 129–138.
   Reprinted in The Sociology of Urban Life: A Text Book with Readings. by T. LYNN SMITH and C. A. MCMAHAN. New York: Dryden Press, 1951, p. 84–97.
   Translated into Russian: "Funktsional'naia Klassifikatsiia gorodov S.Sh.A.," translated by V. M. GOKHMAN, edited by V. V. POKSHISHEVSKII in Geografiia Gorodov. Moskva: Izdatel'stvo "Progress," 1965, p. 121–134.
   Reprinted in Allgemeine Stadtgeographie, edited by PETER SCHÖLLER. Darmstadt: Wissenschaftliche Buchgesellschaft, 1969, p. 289–309.

7. "Suburbs," American Journal of Sociology, vol. 49, no. 1 (July, 1943), p. 1–13.
   Reprinted in Readings in Urban Geography, edited by HAROLD M. MAYER and CLYDE F. KOHN. Chicago: University of Chicago Press, 1959, p. 544–555.

8. "The Cities of the Soviet Union," Geographical Review, vol. 35, no. 1 (January, 1945), p. 107–121.
   Translated in part into Spanish, „Las Ciudades de la Unión Soviética," Revista Geográfica Americana, vol. 23, no. 140 (May, 1945), p. 292–296.

9, "Ethnic Groups in Cities of the Soviet Union," Geographical Review, vol. 35, no. 3 (July, 1945), p. 466–473.

10. "The Ruhr," Scientific Monthly, vol. 60, no. 1 (January, 1945), p. 25–29.

11. "The Nature of Cities," Annals of the American Academy of Political and Social Science, vol. 242 (November, 1945), p. 7–17 (with EDWARD L. ULLMAN). Reprinted in:
Reader in Urban Sociology, edited by PAUL K. HATT and ALBERT J. REISS, JR. GLENCOE, IL: The Free Press, 1951, p. 222–232.
Outside Readings in Geography, edited by FRED E. DOHRS, LAWRENCE M. SOMERS, and DONALD R. PETTERSON. New York: Thomas Y. Crowell, 1955, p. 659–670.
Cities and Society: The Revised Reader in Urban Sociology, edited by PAUL K HATT and ALBERT J. REISS, JR. GLENCOE, IL: The Free Press, 1957, p. 237–247.
Readings in Urban Geography, edited by HAROLD M. MAYER and CLYDE F. KOHN. Chicago: University of Chicago Press, 1959, p. 277–286.
Translated into Russian: "Sushchnost' Gorodov," in: Geografiia Gorodov, translated by V. M. GOKHMAN, edited by V. V. POKSHISHEVSKII. Moskva: Izdatel'stvo "Progress," 1965, p. 255–268.
Bobbs-Merrill Reprint Series in Geography G-85. Indianapolis, IN: Bobbs-Merrill, 1968.
Allgemeine Stadtgeographie, edited by PETER SCHÖLLER. Darmstadt: Wissenschaftliche Buchgesellschaft, 1969, p. 220–237.
A Geography of Urban Places, edited by ROBERT G. PUTNAM, FRANK J. TAYLOR, and PHILIP G. KETTLE. Toronto and London: Methuen, 1970, p. 91–101.
The Sociology of the City, edited by SANDOR HALEBSKY. New York: Charles Scribner's Sons, 1973, p. 102–115.
Comparative Urban Structure: Studies in the Ecology of Cities, edited by KENT P. SCHWIRIAN. Lexington, MA: D. C. Heath, 1974, p. 217–226.

12. "The Ruhr Coal-Mining District," Geographical Review, vol. 36, no. 2 (April, 1946), p. 194–221.

13. "Utilizing the Earth," School Science and Mathematics, vol. 48, no. 3, whole no. 419 (March, 1948), p. 177–182.

14. "Geographic Publications in the United States During World War II (1939–1945), Revista Geográfica do Instituto Pan-Americano de Geografía e Historia, vols. 5–8. nos. 13–24 (1949), p. 117–121.

15. "Geographical Serials," Geographical Review, vol. 40, no. 4 (October, 1950), p. 649–656 (with JEROME D. FELLMANN).

16. "Geographical Literature on the Soviet Union: A Discussion," Geographical Review, vol. 42, no. 4 (October, 1952), p. 615–627.

17. "The Refugee Problem of Germany," Economic Geography, vol. 29, no. 1 (January, 1953), p. 10–25 (with GABRIELE WÜLKER).

18. "The Industrial Resources," chapter 5 in: Soviet Economic Growth: Conditions and Perspectives, edited by ABRAM BERGSON. Evanston, IL: Row Peterson and Co., 1953, p. 163–179.

19. "Geography of Manufacturing," in: American Geography: Inventory and Prospect, edited by PRESTON E. JAMES and CLARENCE F. JONES. Syracuse, NY: Syracuse University Press for the Association of American Geographers, 1954, p. 292–308.
Translated into Russian as „Geografiia Obrabatyvaiushchei Promyshlennosti," in: Amerikanskaia Geografiia. Moskva: Izdatel'stvo Inostrannoi Literatury, 1957, p. 283–299.

18

20. "The Market as a Factor in the Localization of Industry in the United States," Annals of the Association of American Geographers, vol. 44, no. 4 (December, 1954), p. 315–348. Reprinted in:
The Appraisal Journal, vol. 24, no. 1 (January, 1956), p. 57–86.
Business Week, April 3, 1954, p. 60–64 (abridged).
Bobbs-Merrill Reprint Series in Geography G-84. Indianapolis, IN: Bobbs-Merrill, 1968.
Readings in Economic Geography: The Location of Economic Activity, edited by ROBERT H. T. SMITH, EDWARD J. TAAFFE, and LESLIE J. KING. Chicago: Rand McNally and Co., 1968, p. 186–199.

21. "U.S.S.R. Resources: I. Heavy Industry," Focus, vol. 5, no. 6 (February, 1955), 6 p.; revised, vol. 13, no. 5 (January, 1963); revised, vol. 19, no. 6 (February, 1969). Also published in Japanese translation.

22. "U.S.S.R. Resources: II. Agriculture," Focus, vol. 5., no. 9 (May, 1955), 6 p.; revised, vol. 13, no. 7 (March, 1963); revised, vol. 20, no. 4 (December, 1969).

23. "Distorted Maps: A Teaching Device." Journal of Geography, vol. 54, no. 6 (September, 1955), p. 286–289 (with GEORGE B. McDOWELL).

24. "Soviet Agricultural Resources Reappraised," Journal of Farm Economics, vol. 38, no. 2 (May, 1956), p. 258–273.

25. "The Pressure of Residential-Industrial Land Use," in: Man's Role in Changing the Face of the Earth, edited by WILLIAM L. THOMAS, Jr. Chicago: University of Chicago Press, 1956, p. 881–895.

26. "Agricultural Production in the United States: The Past Fifty Years and the Next," Geographical Review, vol. 47, no. 2 (April, 1957), p. 175–193.

27. "Geography in the Soviet Union," Professional Geographer, Vol. 10, no. 1 (January, 1958), p. 8–13.

28. „Geograficheskie Issledovaniia v SShA." (Geographical Research in the United States), Vestnik Akademii Nauk S.S.S.R., 1958, no. 2, p. 23–30 (in Russian).

29. "Geographic Research and Teaching Institutions in the Soviet Union," Erdkunde, Archiv für wissenschaftliche Geographie, vol. 12, no. 3 (1958), p. 214–221.

30. "English, French, German, and Russian as Supplementary Languages in Geographical Serials," Geographical Review, vol. 49, no. 3 (July, 1959), p. 387–405.

31. "The Teaching of Geography in the Soviet Union," Chapter 16 in: New Viewpoints in Geography, edited by PRESTON E. JAMES, 29th Yearbook of the National Council for the Social Studies. Washington, DC: National Council for the Social Studies, 1959, p. 248–257.

32. „Vpechatleniia Inostrannogo Geografa ot Tret'ego S"ezda Geograficheskogo Obshchestva SSSR." (Impressions of a Foreign Geographer of the Third Congress of the Geographical Society of the USSR), Izvestiia Akademii Nauk SSSR, Seriia Geograficheskaia, 1960, no. 3, p. 114–117 (in Russian).

33. "Current Geographical Serials, 1960," Geographical Review, vol. 51, no. 2 (April, 1961), p. 284–289 (with JEROME D. FELLMANN).

34. "Appraisal of Geographic Research and Training Programs in the Soviet Union," Professional Geographer, vol. 14, no. 1 (January, 1962), p. 69–72.
Translated into Russian as „Vyskazyvaniia zarubezhnykh uchenykh o sovetskoi

geografii," Izvestiia Akademii Nauk SSSR, Seriia Geograficheskaia, 1962, no. 4, p. 106–109.

35. "The Land," chapter 2 in: Basic Russian Publications: An Annotated Bibliography on Russia and the Soviet Union, edited by PAUL L. HORECKY. Chicago: University of Chicago Press, 1962, p. 25–48.

36. „Metody issledovanii v oblasti ekonomicheskogo raionirovaniia" (Methods of research in economic regionalization), Izvestiia Akademii Nauk SSSR, Seriia Geograficheskaia, 1963, no. 4, p. 128–136 (in Russian).

37. "Methods of Research in Economic Regionalization," Geographia Polonica, vol. 4 (1964), p. 59–86.

38. "The Land," chapter 3 in: Russia and the Soviet Union: A Bibliographic Guide to Western-Language Publications, edited by PAUL L. HORECKY. Chicago: University of Chicago Press, 1965, p. 46–54.

39. "The Geographic Study of Foreign Areas and Cultures in Liberal Education," in: Geography in Undergraduate Liberal Education, A Report of the Geography in Liberal Education Project. Washington, DC: Association of American Geographers, 1965, p. 25–33.

40. "Geographical Serials of Latin America. Revistas Geográficas de la América Latina," Revista Geográfica (Instituto Panamericano de Geografia e Historia. Commisão de Geografia), no. 64 (June, 1966), p. 148–167 (in English and Spanish). First issued as a separate paper for the Latin American Regional Conference, International Geographical Union, August 3–8, 1966, México, D.F., México.

41. Annotated List of Selected Current Geographical Serials of the Americas and the Iberian Peninsula. Lista Selectica y Anotada de Revistas Geográficas Corrientes de las Américas y la Península Ibérica. Chicago: University of Chicago, Center for International Studies, 1967, 16 p. (in English and Spanish).

42. "City and Region in the Soviet Union," chapter 11 in: Urbanization and its Problems, Essays in Honour of E. W. Gilbert, edited by R. P. BECKINSALE and J. M. HOUSTON. Oxford: Blackwell, 1968, p. 277–303.

43. "Central Places," International Encyclopedia of the Social Sciences. New York Macmillan and the Free Press, 1968, vol. 2, p. 365–370 (with BRIAN J. L. BERRY).

44. "East Germany: The Land," chapter 23 in: East-Central Europe: A Guide to Basic Publications, edited by PAUL L. HORECKY. Chicago: University of Chicago Press, 1969, p. 369–373.

45. "Urbanization and Population Growth in the Soviet Union, 1959–1970," Geographical Review, vol. 61, no. 1 (January, 1971), p. 102–124.

46. „Les Révolutions urbaine et démographique et l'accroissement de la population urbaine en Union Soviétique," Bulletin de l'Association de Géographes Francais, no. 385–386 (janvier-février, 1971), p. 17–32.
Essentially the same paper is available in English:
"The Urban and Demographic Revolutions and Urban Population Growth – the Case of the Soviet Union," in: Urbanization in Europe. Budapest, Hungary: Akadémiai Kiadó, 1975, p. 69–77. European Regional Conference, International Geographical Union, Budapest, Hungary, 1971.

47. "Curent Geographical Serials, 1970," Geographical Review, vol. 63, no. 1 (January, 1973), p. 99–105 (with JEROME D. FELLMANN).

48. "Geographic Studies of the Soviet Union: Some Reflections," chapter 1 in: Geographers Abroad: Essays on the Problems and Prospects of Research in Foreign Areas, edited by MARVIN W. MIKESELL. Chicago: University of Chicago, Department of Geography, Research Paper no. 152, 1973, p. 1−15.

49. "Geography," chapter 3 in Sources of Information in the Social Sciences: A Guide to the Literature, by CARL M. WHITE and associates. 2nd ed., Chicago: American Library Association, 1973, p. 139−180.

50. "Soviet Cities and Trends of Urbanization," in: Urban Geography in Developing Countries, edited by R. L. SINGH. Varanasi, India: The National Geographical Society of India, 1973, p. xxvii-xxxv. Proceedings of the I.G.U. Symposium no. 15, Varanasi, India, November 22−29, 1968, held in connection with the 21st International Geographical Congress, India, 1968.

51. "Geography," in: The International Encyclopedia of Higher Education, edited by ASA S. KNOWLES. San Francisco: Jossey-Bass, 1977, vol. 5, p. 1818−1822.

52. "Patterns of Cities," in: A Man for All Regions: the Contributions of Edward L. Ullman to Geography. Papers of the Fourth Carolina Geographical Symposium. J. D. EYRE, editor. Chapel Hill NC: University of North Carolina at Chapel Hill, Department of Geography, Studies in Geography, no. 11, 1978, p. 66−79.

53. "Geography at Chicago in the 1930s and 1940s," Annals of the Association of American Geographers, vol. 69, no. 1 (March, 1979), p. 21−32.

54. "Current Geographical Serials 1980," Geographical Review, vol. 71, no. 1 (January, 1981), p. 83−90 (with JEROME D. FELLMANN).

55. "The Urban and Industrial Transformation of Japan," Geographical Review, vol. 72, no. 1 (January, 1982), p. 50−89.

56. "Urban Geography in Japan: A Survey of Recent Literature," Urban Geography, vol. 3, no. 1 (January-March, 1982), p. 1−21 (with RICHARD LOUIS EDMONDS).

57. "U.S.S.R.," chapter 9 in: A Guide to Information Sources in the Geographical Sciences, edited by STEPHEN GODDARD. London: Croom Helm; Totowa, NJ: Barnes and Noble, 1983, p. 179−188.

58. "Geography," chapter 3 in: Sources of Information in the Social Sciences: A Guide to the Literature, edited by WILLIAM H. WEBB and associates. 3rd ed. Chicago: American Library Association, 1986, p. 149−212.

59. "Basic Geography," chapter 12 in: The Soviet Union Today: an Interpretive Guide, edited by JAMES CRACRAFT. 2nd ed. Chicago: University of Chicago Press, 1987, p. 137−153. 368. (1st ed., 1983, p. 137−152).

60. "Mongolia," Encyclopaedia Britannica, 1989 and later editions, vol. 24, p. 340−352 (co-author).

61. "Geography," Encyclopaedia Britannica, 1989 and later editions, vol. 19. p. 917−926.

62. "Urban Geography in the United States: My Experience of the Formative Years," Urban Geography, vol. 11, no. 4 (July-August, 1990), p. 403−417.

63. "The Unification of Germany in 1990," Geographical Review, vol. 81, no. 2 (April, 1991), p. 170−182.

64. "Major National Data Sources: USA," in: The Student's Companion to Geography, edited by ANDREW GOUDIE, ALISDAIR ROGERS, and HEATHER VILES. Oxford: Basil Blackwell. In press.

65. "Land, Environment, and People," chapter 2 in: Soviet Studies Guide, edited by Tania Konn. London: Bowker-Saur. In press.

C. Adresses and general articles

1. "Isolationism in the Soviet Union," Proceedings of the Utah Academy of Sciences, Arts and Letters, vol. 27 (1949—1950), p. 37—45.
2. "Growing Food by Decree in Soviet Russia," Foreign Affairs, vol. 33, no. 2 (January, 1955), p. 268—281.
3. "Address of Welcome: 25th Anniversary of the Social Science Research Building, The University of Chicago, November 10, 1955," in: The State of the Social Sciences, edited by LEONARD D. WHITE. Chicago: The University of Chicago Press, 1956, p. 1—8.
4. "Universities and Society in the United States: Democracy and Diversity," in: Universität und Moderne Gesellschaft. Referate und Diskussionsbeiträge zu dem im Sommer 1957 vom Chicago-Ausschuß der Johann Wolfgang Goethe-Univerität in Frankfurt/Main veranstalteten Seminar. Herausgegeben von CHAUNCY D. HARRIS und MAX HORKHEIMER. Frankfurt/Main 1959, p. 30—40.
5. "Society, Science, and Education in the Soviet Union," Proceedings of the National Academy of Sciences, vol. 45, no. 5 (May, 1959), p. 684—692.
6. "The New World of Learning," University of Chicago Magazine, April, 1962, p. 3—5, 8. Convocation Address, The University of Chicago, March, 1962.
7. "Area Studies and Library Resources," Library Quarterly, vol. 35, no. 4 (October, 1965), p. 205—217.
   Reprinted in: Area Studies and the Library, edited by TSUEN-HSUIN TSIEN and HOWARD W. WINGER. Chicago: University of Chicago Press, 1966, p. 3—15.

D. Memorials and appreciations

1. "Robert Swanton Platt (1891—1964)", Geographical Review, vol. 44, no. 3 (July, 1964), p. 444—445.
2. "Charles C. Colby, 1884—1965," Annals of the Association of American Geographers, vol. 56, no. 2 (June, 1966), p. 378—382.
3. "Stephen Sargent Visher, 1887—1967," Journal of Geography, vol. 67, no. 6 (September, 1968), p. 378—379.
4. "Baranskii, Nikolai N." International Encyclopedia of the Social Sciences. New York: Macmillan and the Free Press, 1968, vol. 2, p. 10—12.
5. "Walter Christaller: An Appreciation," Geographical Review, vol. 60, no. 1 (January, 1970), p. 116—119 (with BRIAN J. L. BERRY).
6. "The Work of Many Hands," The University of Chicago Record, vol. 3, no. 8 (December 20, 1974), p. 231—234. The Annual University of Chicago Memorial Service.
7. "Edward Louis Ullman, 1912—1976," Annals of the Association of American Geographers, vol. 67, no. 4 (December, 1977), p. 595—600.

22

8. "Foreword," in: Geography as Spatial Interaction: Edward L. Ullman, edited by RONALD R. BOYCE. Seattle: University of Washington Press, 1980, p. v-xii.
9. "Carl Troll and the International Geographical Union," In Memoriam Carl Troll, by FELIX MONHEIM, WILHELM LAUER, CHAUNCY D. HARRIS. Bonn: Bouvier Verlag Herbert Grundmann, 1980, p. 21–25. Alma Mater: Beiträge zur Geschichte der Universität Bonn, no. 45.
10. "Stephen Barr Jones, 1903–1984," Annals of the Association of American Geographers, vol. 75, no. 2 (June, 1985), p. 271–275.
11. "Theodore Shabad, 1922–1987," Soviet Geography, vol. 28, no. 6 (June, 1987), p. 376–385.
12. "Paul E. Lydolph's Scholarly Contributions to the Climatology and Geography of the Soviet Union," in: Soviet Geography Studies In Our Time. A Festschrift for Paul E. Lydolph, edited by LUTZ HOLZNER and JEANE M. KNAPP. Milwaukee, WI: The College of Letters and Science and The American Geographical Society Collection of the Golda Meir Library, The University of Wisconsin-Milwaukee, 1987, p. 1–21.
13. „Peter Schöller, 1923–1988," Urban Geography, vol. 9, no. 4 (July-August, 1988), p. 393–396.
14. „Alfred H. Meyer, 1893–1988," Journal of Geography, vol. 87, no. 6 (November-December, 1988), p. 236.
15. „Nikolay Ivanovich Vavilov (1887–1943)," Soviet Geography, vol 29, no. 7 (September, 1988), p. 653–657.
16. "Introduction," in: Harold M. Mayer: Fifty Years of Professional Geography, edited by LUTZ HOLZNER and JEANE M. KNAPP. Milwaukee, WI: The American Geographical Society Collection of the Golda Meir Library, The University of Wisconsin-Milwaukee, 1990. p. IX. American Geographical Society Special Publication, no. 2.
17. N. I. Vavilov, 1887–1943," Geographers: Biobibliographical Studies, vol. 13. (1991), p. 117–132.

POLITICAL SYSTEMS AND CITY DEVELOPMENT IN WESTERN SOCIETIES.
A HERMENEUTIC APPROACH

With 3 figures

ELISABETH LICHTENBERGER

Contents

1. Introduction

It is a fascinating task to write a paper on convergences and divergences in urban development in Europe and in Northern America exactly at the time of an overturning of political systems of secular importance. Four and a half decades of post-war development have come to an end, the division of Germany was repealed, the creation of the common European market is a thing of the near future, the vision of a "common house Europe" seems to be within easy reach. Pessimistic fears as to a "eurosclerosis" voiced during the eighties, nurtured on SPENGLER's vision of the decline of The West are forgotten. Up to the turn of the millenium all world fairs will take place in Europe. The "United Nations of Europe" are not just a chimera.

These facts are of importance for future urban development in a number of ways:

1. Gigantic technological projects, such as the "Chunnel", are under way already, new long tunnels under Alpine mountain chains seem to be realizable.

2. A grid system of motorways will be augmented with branches to the east and the south, massive investment into the national networks of railway lines will result in an efficient EC-wide network.

24

3. Densely inhabited urbanized areas, already accommodating a large proportion of the quaternary sector with research and development installations, will profit most from the growth effects.

4. The upper tiers of the national urban systems will be greatly influenced by the supranational power of the common European market. There will be competition among them with respect to newly developing locational advantages, thus creating a sort of "European elite" among the big metropolitan areas.

5. Regional politics in the European Communities will not only change Europe's economic map, but will create a new stratum of "regional centres" that will be identical with the capitals of the Bundesländer in the Federal Republic of Germany only.

6. There is no way to say yet whether and, if so, to what extent the institutionalized instruments for a levelling of social and spatial disparities developed in the social welfare states will remain intact, to what extent social politics will be separated from economic politics and to what extent social politics will be further nationalized as were housing politics in the post-war period.

This question links up with the topic of "convergences and divergences in urban development".

2. Convergences and Divergences in Urban Development

Supporters of the theory of a convergence in urban development and in the development of city systems may quote a number of invariant factors. Among them there are:

1. all of the technologies applied in building, in producing commodities, in transport, in the supply and waste disposal sector, in the fields of communication and information,

2. the economic parameters of a differentiation in the process of a division of labour from the secondary to the tertiary and the quaternary sectors.

Those convinced of a divergence in urban development might name the following variant complexes:

1. persistent structures in urban development, such as the physical structure and land use classes, traditional norms and behaviour on the part of the population and the institutionalized factual and spatial forms of organization,

2. the formal principles of city planning, especially the building types for housing, and

3. the actual political systems with their models and sets of measures for spatial organization and structuring of both the society and economy. This paper focusses on the effects of political systems.

3. Political Systems and Urban Development

3.1 Urban Development, Urban Decay, and Urban Redevelopment

Political systems are tied up with specific processes in the development of the physical structure within the urban area and in the spatial organization of the society. Therefore, each change in the political system results in displacements and a restructuring in the building stock and in the urban society.

In this context, urban development is not taken to be a unilinear process, but is considered a two-way process of urban expansion and urban redevelopment, with growth in general and, therefore, expansion of the urban system always preceding urban redevelopment. The time-lag between expansion and redevelopment of the physical structure is directly dependent on the extent of the investment deficit in the older built-up area (cf. Figure 1).

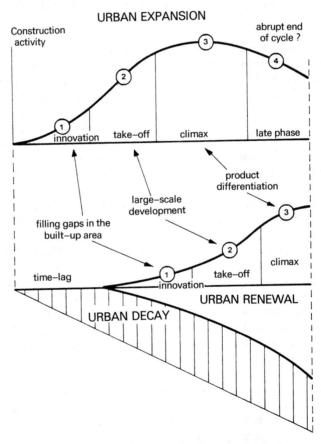

Fig. 1: The dual cycle model of urban redevelopment and urban expansion

At present, urban decay in all of the western world as well as in Europe's eastern countries is marked by a loss of the equilibrium between expansion and redevelopment, with the former being favoured at the expense of the latter.

Below an attempt is made to discuss the problem of urban decay and urban redevelopment against the background of urban growth within different political systems creating similarities or differences.

When comparing urban development in North America and in Europe, three types of political systems are to be considered:
– private capitalism,
– state capitalism and
– concepts of the social welfare state.

3.2. Urban Decay and Urban Redevelopment in Private Capitalism. The Example of the USA

Let us discuss North America first. But for a short period of colonial dependence, urban development in North America was guided by liberalism. Consequently the real estate market was regulated by demand and supply, with the price of land, ground rents and land speculation being the regulatives.

As there was hardly any change in the political system for the past 200 years, the cities of North America could be considered model cases for the effects of capitalistic rules on urban systems when interacting with simultanous changes in the technologies of manufacturing, building, and transport.

The elements listed below may help to understand this type of urban development:

1. The accepted social norms are characterized by pursuit of profits and maximizing of gains. This attitude controls the investment strategies of the population and prevents any investment into buildings that does increase their market value. Especially banks and insurance companies place their investments where high yields are to be expected, therefore overshadowed areas in the inner cities tend to be redlined as "written off zones". Even if some people were ready to renovate decaying objects, they would not be granted loans. For this reason, urban redevelopment within the framework of the process of a pointedly economy-oriented recycling can only consist either in a complete demolishing of former residential areas, replacing them by traffic routes and junctions or other nonresidential functions, or a gentrification of aesthetically attractive sections in historical styles for an affluent new city population.

2. The extraordinarily high rate of housing construction together with a rapid progress in technology has shortened the average life-span of housing structures, so that it corresponds to the human life-span or, most recently, equals one generation only. Consequently, all new buildings soon become part of the grey zone of overshadowed or blighted areas. Therefore, house-ownership is being

27

defined according to the actual housing needs of, and economic benefit for, an individual or a household, but is of little importance in any property transfer through inheritance.

3. An extremely high mobility of both labour and capital is required by the continous adaptation to the market. Capital is quickly withdrawn wherever it does not yield profits. Nobody considers vacant buildings an eyesore as no individual or group feels responsible for a neat appearance of parts of the city outside its immediate neighbourhood. Mobility on the labour market is a matter of course in the social behaviour set of a promotion-oriented society.

4. As the public sector has at its disposal a very small proportion of the budget only, measures to prevent a further expansion of physical decay cannot be financed from public funds. Moreover a society dominated by middle classes convinced of the merits of private capitalism strongly opposes any augmentation of the general social overhead. This attitude contributes to a further progress of the processes of decay, segregation and marginalization, and furthers enlargement of the areas affected.

5. The taxation system is of utmost importance for the processes of decay. Taxes levied on land form the basis for the budgets of the local authorities and, thus, for the financing of social benefits. Therefore, there is no escape from the vicious spiral of marginal population – few taxable assets – modest tax revenue – low-quality public institutions, such as schools and hospitals etc.

During the fifties the extent of urban decay in the USA was recorded for the first and only time. Within the framework outlined above it has reached an extent in the inner cities that is almost beyond the grasp of a European. Feedback-effects of the enormous growth of surburbs in the Metropolitan Areas on the inner cities make themselves felt in all functional sectors:

1. There was a marked decline in many CBDs. The huge extent of commercial blight was described for the first (and last!) time by B.J.L. BERRY for Chicago in 1963. Ever since, this process has somehow been left out of account both by the general public and by research into urban problems.

2. When industry was relocated and reorganized, massive decay set in in the inner industrial belt around the downtowns (industrial blight). During the past decades many of these extensive areas of vacant industrial premises and neglected open spaces were cleared and then occupied by motorways.

3. Residential blight and slum formation are, however, among those phenomena taking up most space. Within these "inner city deserts" of the late industrial and postindustrial society property values have dropped to zero, and despite a state-initiated frontier-movement granting ownership of a vacant building to any interested party for a nominal sum of one dollar, decay of housing keeps progressing aground the CBDs. In Philadelphia, e. g., there is a ring of decay 5 to 10 kilometres wide, with about 40.000 vacant houses (cf. Figure 2).

Urban redevelopment as a public obligation is an unsolved, seemingly repressed problem. Private investors have been concentrating on two tasks since

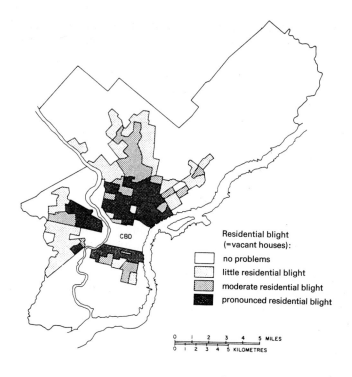

Residential blight
(=vacant houses):

no problems

little residential blight

moderate residential blight

pronounced residential blight

Source: L. S. Bourne, 1981:183.

Fig. 2: Decaying residential areas in Philadelphia

the late sixties: downtown-redevelopment and gentrification.

Downtown-redevelopment by means of replacing the existing building stock by skyscrapers providing office space for enterprises of the tertiary and quaternary sectors, mainly banks and insurance companies and other highly specialized economic services, mirrors the rapidly increasing importance of these economic sectors. Recently a growing number of small households of white members of the middle classes, mostly young, often single professional people with comfortable incomes, tend to consider the downtowns as ideal situations for housing. The boom of gentrification – optimistically lauded up to the early eighties – has, however, subsided, and though it affected the large Metropolitan Areas it did not spread to lower strata in the urban hierarchy.

The phenomenon of counterurbanization often discussed during the seventies has not come to a standstill yet. A "production" of capital by means of speculation in, and increases in the price of, land due to a close interaction of car manufacturers, oil firms, large organizations of the building industry, banks providing mortages and companies engaged in highway construction has turned suburbanization into a self-regulating process. Suburbia has become the most prominent element in the settlement system of the USA.

Against the background of the large distances covered when moving and an almost incredible extent of mobility it is a fascinating phenomenon that there still is a very marked process of demographic, social, and ethnic segregation going on. As areas suitable for settlements are a nearly ubiquitous resource, neither people nor authorities seem to have realized that "abandoned centres" are developing in the North American cities – and no one considers introducing measures to stop this development.

The preference for a "suburban way of life" is based on an anti-urban attitude that is, however, not only an outcome of the general accessibility of modern forms of communication, of goods and services made possible by the diffusion of technological progress, but results from the historical and political fact that the basic concept of Continental European urban development, that of the "burghers community" and of the important status group of the burghers in a preindustrial society (cf. M. WEBER's "Society and Economy"), did not influence North American urban development.

3.3. Urban Decay and Urban Redevelopment in State Capitalism

Let us consider the (former) system of state capitalism in the countries in Eastern Europe now. Interestingly enough, large areas of decay can be found in all of the inner cities there as well. There are, however, basic differences to the system of private capitalism. Above all there is a strict allocation system of the centralized urban development politics without any kind of market system regulating the ratio between capital, labour force, and production output. Because of the nationalization of land, there is no possibility of producing capital by means of an increase of land values. The state, its economy and its population are forced to manage without capitalizing land as an economic resource.

As the laws of a market economy are not operative, very complicated grey and black markets came into existence. Thus, a market of exchange deals is characteristic of state capitalism and holds true for the housing sector as a whole as well as for specific consumption goods and services. Housing is a scarce resource. The public allocation system forces the applicants to wait for several years before they are assigned an apartment. In this way the population is immobilized. There are further consequences, such as paradox discrepancies between the state of repair of dwellings and the social status of their inhabitants. Whereas areas of decay house marginal social and ethnic groups in the cities of capitalistic states, this is not true for the cities of the – so far – socialist countries. Only in the course of a succession of generations phenomena of marginalization

30

tend to appear to a certain extent, but they are counteracted by the public allocation policy in the housing sector, as anti-segregation strategies are implicitly included into the allocation system.

Recent political developments in the former COMECON countries have probably put an end to the urban development politics that could be characterized in the following way: Public and social institutions have absolute priority over the private sphere. They are concentrated in imposing new city centres of "socialist urban design", whereas the "bourgeois old towns" and the blocks of flats of the Founders' Period* were left to decay. Budapest provides an especially impressive example for this fact. The area of "urban redevelopment" comprises about 120.000 apartments that should be renovated or demolished within one generation, that is up to 2015. The location of the blighted areas, namely in most cases in the vicinity of the city centres, in the countries in Eastern Europe parallels the situation in North America (cf. Figure 3).

3.4. Urban Decay and Urban Redevelopment in Social Welfare States

With respect to the spatial pattern and development of urban decay and urban redevelopment the social welfare states of Western Europe occupy an intermediate position, though there are considerable variations among them due to differences in the respective national housing politics. A few features common to all are listed below:

1. There are segmented markets for housing, working, and leisure activities, i. e. certain segments in the supply of apartments, jobs, and leisure facilities have been removed from the market – either due to specific property rights (government property, property of local authorities, cooperatives etc.) or legal limitations of their marketability. Furthermore there are subsidies granted for specific objects or groups of individuals. Moreover there are important regulations as to the siphoning off of speculation profits on land. Land-use tends to be strictly regulated, and especially in city centres laws as to the protection of historical buildings severely limit construction activities.

2. The segmentation of the housing market is one of those factors of urban development the importance of which cannot be overrated. Basically the individual segments have different conditions of access:

(1) There are privileged groups (members of political parties, employees of certain enterprises, certain professions etc.) that are given access to apartments at a price lower than the market value.

(2) Laws and ordinances reduce the landlords' power over their possessions, and tenement protection laws furnish the tenants with a sort of "pseudo-ownership" of their apartments.

---

* Founders' Period = Period between 1848 and 1914

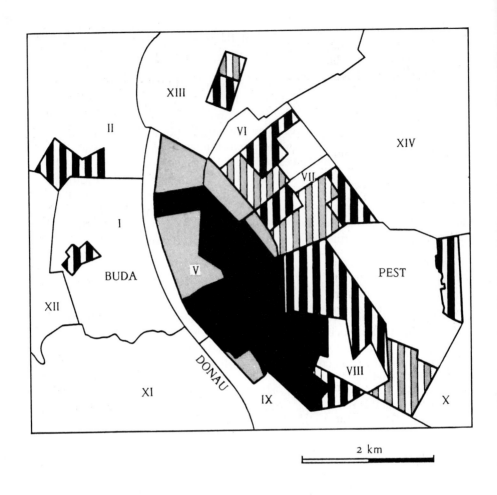

complete renewal 1985–2000

renovation 1985–2000

complete renewal 2000–2015

renovation 2000–2015

Source: Office for Urban Renewal Budapest VII

Fig. 3: Urban Decay and urban redevelopment in Budapest

(3) In accordance with the prevalent ideology, housing politics is being used as an instrument for an anti-segregation strategy in certain countries, and in some cities as a means for achieving an effect comparable to gerrymandering.

3. Furthermore it is an extremely important fact that, for a long time, the state administration or the local authorities have been providing institutions and networks of the technical and social infrastructures in all of the welfare states. Special importance is to be attached to education politics and the integration of different social and ethnic groups by means of a general public school system, thus, more or less, eliminating the influence of private educational institutions.

Urban decay as a scientific construct and as a physical feature is almost unknown in Northern Europe and can hardly be found in the Federal Republic of Germany and in Switzerland. In Germany, it was mainly the building stock at present threatened by decay elsewhere that was destroyed by bombing or fighting during, and at the end of, World War II. Moreover there is a long and well-established tradition of regulations and measures with respect to a conservation and/or renewal of the physical structure of cities. It was the municipal authorities in the late 19th century that carried out a sanitation of older parts of the cities by introducing modern infrastructure.

As early as at the turn of the century, moreover, the conservation movement succeeded in starting to protect historical and cultural monuments in the German-speaking countries. A demolition and complete redevelopment of (large parts of) the downtowns – a procedure quite common in Great Britain first in the Founders' Period and then again during the sixties – did not take place there, but conservation of the old towns and preservation of historical and cultural monuments were combined into a conservative ideology of urban design, later on adopted by France with its "Lex Malraux", too.

3.5. Political Systems and Urban Decay

A comparison of cities in diverse countries shows that urban decay is common to all political systems of the Western Hemisphere. Its main cause seems to consist in the development of a disproportion between urban expansion and urban renewal. The scheme below presents an outline of the main features.

In North America, the exodus of inhabitants from the central cities created a new settlement system: suburbia. It is due to suburbanization that more than one half of the US population is living in this independent socioeconomic system at present. These suburbanites are, however, not aware of the problems of the central cities. There, a very complex vicious spiral of lacking reinvestment in the physical structure, decreasing tax returns, and marginalization of the population has resulted in extensive central blight areas (cf. above).

Even a return of some of the population in connection with gentrification and an adaptation and renewal of older areas of terraced houses in the inner cities in

PROCESSES IN URBAN DEVELOPMENT

North America	COMECON Countries
exodus from the cities	migration to the cities
suburbanization	urban expansion
counterurbanization	second homes movement,
	splitting up of housing function

DECAY OF THE PHYSICAL STRUCTURES

decay of the building stock of the Founders' Period

decay in older suburbs

REDEVELOPMENT

return to the central city	regrouping of population
of new city dwellers	migration to the cities continuing
gentrification	urban renewal in old town

their historical style could not stop the progress of decay. Only in a few large cities the take-off of the quaternary sector triggered a complete redevelopment – Atlanta is one of them.

Urban decay must, however, be considered as both a state and a process. The latter is governed by the general laws of innovation, therefore, on the one hand, ever younger housing is affected and, on the other hand, the process expands from the centre towards the periphery. Thus, having started in the areas built-up during the Founders' Period, it can now be observed already in older suburbs and small towns on the fringe of the large agglomerations.

Interestingly enough, there is a similar development in the cities of countries with a state capitalism in Eastern Europe. There urban decay is caused by a lack of reinvestment in the building stock too, for different reasons, though. Many of the former houseowners were expropriated, and many of the houses are government property still. Moreover the low-rents policy left house-owners without funds for investing into their apartment houses. National budgets could not provide for both urban expansion and urban redevelopment. Especially in the new provinces of the Federal Republic of Germany blight of the former "bourgeois" old towns is marked, also due to the ideology concerning urban design prevalent for one and a half generations that insisted on the necessity of creating new socialist cities.

This points to fundamental differences: There was no urban exodus and no suburbanization in the socialist countries. Because of the unfavourable conditions in rural areas and in the small towns people tend to move into cities, especially large ones. Suburbanization and counterurbanization are substituted

34

by a division of the housing function. Publicly subsidized housing in large blocks of flats combined with low-rents politics brought about a feature singular to Europe, namely a bipartition of the housing function with separate units for working and for leisure (in the USSR: dachas). Thus sections of the urban population are "living in two societies". It is mainly in the (formerly) socialist countries and in some large cities in Western Europe, where politics of low rents have somehow "subsidized" the acquiring and upkeep of second homes. In France, Sweden, Austria, Hungary and the CSFR one third of the inhabitants of the large cities have two residences. The consequences of this phenomenon cannot be discussed here. Let it suffice to say that this lebensform has become an important criterium for evaluating the social prestige of an individual and is considered a need by large segments of the society. The new life style has become independent from the political framework within which it originated, and this is true of the situation in the former COMECON countries, too.

The second type of the phenomenon of a "life in two societies" is to be found with guestworkers who have come to work in the inner cities in Northwestern Europe. The life-style they have developed is an ambivalent one – and far too little attention has been paid to this fact so far: In their places of origin, mainly small rural settlements and towns in Portugal, Spain, Italy, Yugoslavia and Greece, they have become an upper stratum of society. Thus, the European counterpart of counterurbanization in America consists in the existence of a large number of second homes on the one hand and the building activities of the guestworkers in their countries of origin on the other hand.

4. Future Developments

4.1. The Problem of Recycling the Physical Structure of the City

Due to the progress in all fields of knowledge, technology, and capital, the "period of decay" of almost all material and immaterial goods tends to shorten irrevocably. When applying this concept to the physical structure of cities it signifies the reduction in the average life-span of all physical structures, especially a rapidly increasing outdatedness of the fabric of buildings, wherever massive construction activities, as e. g. in the USA, will reproduce the present building stock within a period of 40 years if the present rate is retained. With the rapid rate of rotation of the capital invested in the technical infrastructure, industrial and office premises as well as residential buildings the physical structure of cities loses its stabilizing function in the sequence of generations in the urban society.

Two developments are blended: a decrease in the average life-span of specific elements of the physical structure and an increase in that of the urban population. The generally accepted rule up to the present of persistent building structures surviving the succession of generations is no longer valid. A new immanent problem came into existence: Extensive decay of many elements of the urban physical structure is the counterpart of growth.

"Permanent recycling" is not only to replace traditional waste disposal but must be applied to all elements of the physical structure of cities too.

Migration studies show that immigration waves encumber the social system with a sort of "mortgage of death" one or two generations later – a similar concept could be applied to the fabric of cities. Today's construction rates can be used to estimate tomorrow's recycling needs. Urban planning must be re-oriented: land-use changes in the recent past should be the basis for a prognosis of future trends in land-use successions.

4.2. Back to Urbanity

Sociologists, architects, and cultural historians have been discussing urbanity. Urbanity is a theoretical construct, but an ideology too. The theoretical construct comprises material elements of the built urban culture as well as organizational elements of the urban society and features of a specific life-style. It was, however, not operationalized, not translated into a model and not calibrated.

As to the physical structure of a city, monumental buildings, large open spaces, and capacious traffic arteries, a demonstration of grandeur and diversity are indispensable features of urbanity, as are a wide range of life-styles, with a possibility of highly individual forms of dwelling, of perception and learning potentials, and a broad spectrum as to goods of all descriptions offered.

A hypothesis might be formulated: Urbanity cannot dispense with demographic integration. To my mind, this condition is extremely important: if there is segregation according to age-groups and household types, if the "cohorts seem to return to separate quarters", the societal continuum breaks up with respect to the passing on of cultural traditions and, thus, urbanity. The important function of the large households of the upper and middle classes for the thriving of urban culture and urban lebensforms can be deduced from a study of pre-industrial urban culture.

I do hope that the segregration model prevalent in North America, with families living in suburbs and small households being concentrated in the inner cities, will never be valid in Europe, and that young people will want to settle – as can be observed in some places already – in the inner cities. In this way the large cities will be able to survive as lively innovation centres of European culture.

Bibliography (selected):

APPLEYARD, D., 1979. The Conservation of European Cities. The MIT Press, Cambridge, Mass. and London: 8−275.

BEAUREGARD, R. A., 1988. Urban restructuring in comparative perspective. In: R. A. BEAUREGARD (ed.). Atop the Urban Hierarchy. Rowman and Littlefield, Totowa, N. J.

BERGER, G. E., 1967. The concept and causes of urban blight. Land Economics 42: 369−383.

BERRY, B. J. L., 1985. Islands of revewal in seas of decay. In: P. PETERSEN (ed). The New Urban Reality. Brooking Institution, Washington, D.C.: 69−96.

BERRY, B. J. L., R. J. TENANT and B. J. GARNER, 1963. Commercial structure and commercial blight, retail patterns and processes in the city of Chicago. Research Paper 85, Dept. of Geography, University of Chicago.

BORGHORST, H., 1987. Citizen Participation in Urban Renewal in Berlin (West). In: C. S. YADAV (ed.). Slums, Urban Decline and Revitalization. Perspectives in Urban Geography VII. Concept Publishing Company, New Delhi.

BOULDING, K. E., 1963. The death of the city: a frightened look at post-civilization. In: O. HANDLIN and J. BURCHARD (eds.). The Historian and the City. MIT-Press, Cambridge, Mass.: 133−145.

BOURNE, L. S., 1980. Alternative perspectives on urban decline and population deconcentration. Urban Geography I: 39−52.

BÖVENTER, E. von, 1979. Urban Decay as a Process. CES Conference Series 21: 481−508.

BURTENSHAW, D. und B. CHALKLEY, 1990. Urban decay and rejuvenation. In: D. PINDER and J. DAWSON (eds.). Western Europa − Challenge and Change. Belhaven Press, London.

CHESHIRE, P. C., G. CARBONARO and D. HAY, 1986. Problems of urban decline and growth in EEC countries: or measuring degrees of elephantness. Urban Studies 23,2: 131−151.

CHOATE, P. and S. WALTERS, 1983. America in Ruins: The Decaying Infrastructure. Duke, Durham, N. C.

CORTIE, C. and J. VAN DE VAN, 1981. "Gentrification": keert de woonelite terngnaar de stad? TESG 15,5: 429−446.

CYBRIWSKY, R. A. and J. WESTERN, 1982. Revitalizing downtowns: by whom and for whom? In: D. T. HERBERT and R. J. JOHNSTON (eds.). Geography and the urban environment. John Wiley, Chichester: 343−365.

DAVID, J. and T. KISS, 1984. Ruin and reconstruction of the existing buildings. Maintenance issues of large panel buildings in Hungary. Symposium Industrialized Concrete Structures of Residential and Public Buildings. Papers 2 (= Institute for Building Science Bulletin 78), Budapest: 33−41 and 117−129.

DEAR, M. J.,1976. Abandoned Housing. In: J. S. ADAMS (ed.). Urban Policy-Making and Metropolitan Dynamics: A Comparative Geographical Analysis. Cambridge, Mass.: 59−99.

DUMSDAY, J. 1985. Conference report: Declining cities: who is to blame? Falling apart: what is happening to our cities? The Town and Country Planning Association Annual Conference, London, 6−7 December 1984. Cities 2, 2: 176−178.

ECONOMIC COMMISSION FOR EUROPE (ECE) (ed.), 1983. Urban renewal. Issue paper on area-based improvement prepared by the delegation of Sweden. Vol. 12, Geneva.

ECONOMIC COMMISSION FOR EUROPE (ECE) (ed.), 1985. Urban renovation as part of a global policy in France. Vol. 13, Geneva.

EINEM, E. von, 1987. Comparing Urban Revitalization in the United States and West Germany. In: C. S. YADAV (ed.). Slums, Urban Decline and Revitalization. Perspectives in Urban Geography VII. Concept Publishing Company, New Delhi.

FASSBINDER, H. and E. KALLE, 1982. A comparative study of urban renewal policy. The Netherlands National Committee for the European Urban Renaissance Campaign. Rotterdam.

FRIEDMAN, A., 1983. Social relations at work and the generation of inner city decay. In: J. ANDERSON, S. DUNCAN and R. HUDSON (eds.). Redundant Spaces in Cities and Regions: Studies in Industrial Decline and Social Change. Institute of British Geographers, Special Publication 15.

GALE, D. E., 1984. Neighbourhood Revitalization and the Postindustrial City: A Multinational Perspective. Lexington Books, Lexington, Mass.

GIBSON, M. S. and M. J. LANGSTAFF, 1982. An introduction to urban renewal. (British policy from the 1960s to the present). Hutchinson, London.

GOTTDIENER, M., 1987. The decline of urban politics: political theory and the crisis of the local state. Sage Library of Social Research. Beverly Hills, Cal.

GOTTDIENER, M. 1985. Symposium: whatever happened to the urban crisis? Urban Affairs Quarterly 20, 4.

HALL, P., 1987. Urban Growth and Decline in Western Europe. In: M. DOGAN and J. D. KASARDA (eds.). The Metropolis Era 1. A World of Giant Cities. Sage Publications, London.

KRUMM, R. J. and R. J. VAUGHAN, 1976. The economics of urban blight. The Rand Paper Series, Santa Monica, Cal.

LANG, M. H. 1982. Gentrification amid urban decline: strategies for America's older cities. Cambridge, Mass.

LASKA, S. B. and D. SPAIN (eds.). 1980. Back to the City: Issues in Neighborhood Renovation. New York.

LEVEN, Ch. L. et al., 1976. Neighborhood change: lessons in the dynamics of urban decay. Praeger Special Studies in U.S. Economic, Social, and Political Issues, New York.

LEVINE, M. V., 1987. Downtown redevelopment as an urban growth strategy: a critical appraisal of Baltimore renaissance. Journal of Urban Affairs 9,2.

LEVY, J. P., 1987. The Rehabilitation of Town Centres and Old Quarters/Neighbourhoods in France: Rationality and Interpretations Using the Example of Toulouse. In: C. S. YADAV (ed.). Slums, Urban Decline and Revitalization. Perspectives in Urban Geography VII. Concept Publishing Company, New Delhi.

LEY, D., 1980. Liberal ideology and the post-industrial city. Annals of the Association of American Geographers 80: 238−258.

LICHTENBERGER, E., 1970. The Nature of European Urbanism. Geoforum 4: 45−62.

LICHTENBERGER, E., 1976. The Changing Nature of European Urbanization. In: B. J. L. BERRY (ed.). Urbanization and Counterurbanization. Urban Affairs Annual Reviews 11: 81−107.

LICHTENBERGER, E., 1987. Guestworkers – Life in two Societies. (with H. FASSMANN, EDP-technology). In: G. GLEBE and J. O'LOUGHLIN (eds.). Foreign Minorities in Continental European Cities. Erdkundliches Wissen 84: 240−257.

LICHTENBERGER, E., 1987. Zweitwohnungen im Stadtumland. Berliner Geographische Arbeiten, Sonderheft 4 (Jubiläumskonferenz 1986 der Sektion Geographie der Humboldt-Universität zu Berlin): 68–74.

LICHTENBERGER, E., 1987. Perspectives of Urban Geography. In: Recherches de Géographie urbaine. Hommage au Professeur J. A. Sporck, tome 1: 105–129. Presses Universitaires de Liege, Liege.

LICHTENBERGER, E., 1990. Stadtverfall und Stadterneuerung. Beiträge zur Stadt- und Regionalforschung, Band 10. Verlag der Österreichischen Akademie der Wissenschaften, Wien.

LICHTENBERGER, E. (ed. together with G. HEINRITZ), 1986. The Take-off of Suburbia and the Crisis of the Central City. Proceedings of the International Symposium in Munich and Vienna 1984. Erdkundliches Wissen 76.

LICHTENBERGER, E. and G. HEINRITZ, 1986. Munich and Vienna – A Cross-national Comparison. In: Proceedings of the International Symposium in Munich and Vienna 1984. Erdkundliches Wissen 76: 1–29.

LIPTON, G. S., 1987. The Future Central City: Gentrified or Abandoned? In: C. S. YADAV (ed.). Slums, Urban Decline and Revitalization. Perspectives in Urban Geography VII. Concept Publishing Company, New Delhi.

LONDON, B. and J. PALEN, 1984. Gentrification, Displacement and Neighborhood Revitalization. State University, Albany, New York.

MARCUSE, P., 1986. Abandonment, Gentrification, and Displacement. The Linkages in New York City. In: N. SMITH and P. WILLIAMS (eds.). Gentrification of the City. London and Sydney: 153–177.

MARCUSE, P., 1987. The Decline of Cities in the United States: Inevitable or Deliberate? In: C. S. YADAV (ed.). Slums, Urban Decline and Revitalisation. Perspectives in Urban Geography VII. Concept Publishing Company, New Delhi.

MCKEAN, C., 1977. Fight blight: a practical guide to the causes of urban dereliction and what people can do about it. Kaye & Ward, London.

MEDHURST, F., and J. P. LEWIS, 1969. Urban decay: an analysis and a policy. Macmillan, London.

ROSE E. A. (ed.), 1986. New roles for old cities. Anglo-American policy on declining urban regions. Gower, Aldershot.

ROSENTHAL, D. B. (ed.), 1980. Urban Revitalization. Sage Publications, Beverly Hills, Cal.

SMITH, N. and P. WILLIAMS (eds.), 1984. Gentrification, housing and the restructuring of urban space. Croom Helm, London.

THOMAS, A. D., 1986. Housing and urban renewal: residential decay and revitalisation in the private sector. Urban and Regional Studies 12.

THOMPSON, F. M. L. (ed.), 1982. The rise of suburbia. Themes in Urban History. Leicester University Press, Leicester.

VAN DEN BERG, L. and L. H. KLAASEN, 1978. The process of urban decline. Working Paper 6. Netherlands Economic Institute, Rotterdam.

WEGENER, M., 1982. Modelling urban decline – a multilevel economic-demographic model for the Dortmund region. International Regional Science Review 7: 217–241.

WEGENER, M., 1986. Modelling the Life Cycle of Industrial Cities: A Case Study of Dortmund, Germany. Paper presented at the International Seminar on Economic

Change and Urbanization Trends within Medium Size Metropolitan Systems in Europe, IRPET, Firenze: 18–19 December 1986.

WHITE, P., 1984. The West European City. A Social Geography. Longman, London and New York.

YADAV, C. S. (ed.), 1987. Slums, Urban Decline and Revitalization. Perspectives in Urban Geography VII. Concept Publishing Company, New Delhi.

AREAL PATTERNS OF CITIES TROUGH TIME AND SPACE: TECHNOLOGY AND CULTURE (THE NATURE OF CITIES FURTHER CONSIDERED)

CHAUNCY D. HARRIS

In an effort to model internal patterns within cities and areal distribution of systems of cities, EDWARD L. ULLMAN and I nearly half a century ago wrote a brief paper, "The Nature of Cities" (HARRIS and ULLMAN 1945). The reception of this modest article was far more widespread and more enduring than either of us anticipated at that time. I shall first briefly summarize these models, then make some more extended comments on modifications of these models through time and space. Changes through time reflected particularly evolving technologies. Differences over space reflect particularly culture in its broadest sense.

With respect to internal patterns within cities three models were recognized: concentric rings, as proposed by ERNEST W. BURGESS and the Chicago School of Sociology, sectors as recognized by HOMER HOYT, the Chicago economist, and multiple nuclei, as suggested by ULLMAN and me, both of whom had been students at Chicago. These models were based primarily on American cities, particularly Chicago, in the late 19th and early 20th century in a period of rapid growth and massive European immigration. But as HANS BÖHM has reported similar models had been proposed in Germany much earlier.

In the concentric ring model distance from the city center is a key factor. Outward from the city center density of population and land values decrease but quality of housing and socioeconomic status increase. As the city expands successive waves of new immigrants locate in densely packed older low-quality housing near the center and with time move outward. Individual points go through a sequence or succession of waves of different ethnic or social groups.

In the sector model, once a particular sector, often defined by access along a transport route outward from the center, has acquired a definite character, be it industrial, commercial, high-quality residential, low-quality residential, or other, it tends to preserve that character as land use expands outward along this wedge or sector. These sectors develop at different rates. Typically expansion is most rapid along the axis of high quality housing, resulting in assymetrical patterns. Interstices between sectors along radial transport lines may be be left undeveloped for long periods.

In the multiple nuclei model in American cities different land uses have attachment to different facilities: retail trade and office functions to transport access from the urban area by commuter train, underground lines, streetcar, bus, or private car; wholesale trade and manufacturing, to access to railroad freight shipments; particular ethnic communities to previous immigrants of the same group, churches, schools, and a network of friends, relatives, and diverse organizations that give the community cohesion.

In European cities government, commerce, industry, and church often have different points of attachment. The government center of castle, palace, or city hall may be in one place, the market in another, the central church or cathedral in yet another, and industrial districts in still others. London, England, provides a good example. Westminster is the government center. The City is the commercial center. For many centuries it was physically separated from Westminster by open country crossed by a pleasant walk along the Strand. Canterbury, still farther away, is the religious center. Several industrial areas within and on the edge of London reflect the impact of the Industrial Revolution. Each of these focal points of different activities was historically and areally distinct. Each other major city has its own juxtaposition or separation of city hall, market, church, and industry.

With respect to external patterns in the areal distribution of systems of cities, three types were distinguished: central places, hierarchically organized and evenly spaced in a two-dimensional plane, first rigorously studied by WALTER CHRISTALLER (1933), the German geographer, transportation centers in a one-dimensional linear spacing, and specialized function cities arranged in clustered patterns in areas of special resources, ranging from coalfields for industry to amenities for recreation.

In the search for ever higher levels of generalization one could note a certain commonality of these internal and external models of cities. Three types of geometrical designs occur: a point pattern with distance from a center in the concentric ring model of internal patterns and of central places in urban networks, of linear patterns in sectors in internal structures and in transport alignments in urban networks, and of clustering patterns around differentiated nodes in multiple nuclei internally in cities and in closely spaced groups of specialized cities in urban networks.

Now it is time to make some observations about these models. First, three small notes and then two more extensive discussions. The three notes are on the modification of the models to take into account the complexity of the geographic landscape, density of population, and results of statistical testing in specific cities and areas.

First, the model assumed a homogenous plane. As geographers well know, indeed it is a major object of their study, the earth's surface is wonderfully variegated with irregularities in distribution of virtually all physical and human features and in their particular associations in specific places. Internal and external patterns are substantially modified by location of mountains, hills, slopes, rivers, coastlines, drainage, fertility of the soil, presence of mineral resources, vegetation, historical evolution of settlement, political organization, transport lines, and many other factors.

Second, the model did not deal with size or density of population, which are reflected in the spacing of the internal and external patterns of cities. In areas with lower density of population, central places of the same rank in the hierarchy are more widely spaced and are smaller in size than in areas of high density of population. Periodic markets are one organizational device to make higher-order goods more widely available in areas of low density of population or low demand for a particular good or service. An international group of scholars under the leadership of ROBERT H. T. SMITH, of Australia, and ERDMANN GORMSEN, of Germany (1978, 1979, 1982), have greatly enlarged our understanding of this spatial institution, especially well developed in the Third World.

Third, the model was a simple typology, an ideal paradigm, based on a limited number of observations, not a law, rule, or a regularity developed out of a rigorous statistical analysis of a large body of data. Central-place theory has been the subject of literally hundreds of investigations and interpretations but these cannot be reviewed here. Suffice it to mention the summary of theory and practice by BRIAN J. L. BERRY and colleagues (1988).

The concept of multiple nuclei has been extended well beyond our original concept and applied also in statistical studies of social segregation in American cities, particularly by sociologists and urban geographers. Such studies of communities within cities depend on an available substantial base of statistical data for many social and economic variables by small areal units. Such studies have been developed particularly in Great Britain and the United States.

So much for the three notes. We now turn our attention to two major discussions, one on the historical factor of evolution of urban patterns over time, the other on the areal factor one encounters as one travels from one cultural realm to another. These are questions of modification of the models over time and space.

Historical Dimensions

The growth of cities is a stochastic process in which the structures from earlier epochs form the foundation for the growth in the next. Cities do not develop on a *tabula rasa*, or blank slate, but as modifications and expansions on an existing physical foundation of the built environment, or in a different metaphor as new branches on an existing tree trunk. Of course, the date of major urban expansion leaves its handprint in patterns and structures that reflect the technology and ideals of that period, and which form the base on which later and different patterns are superimposed with modifications, particularly in older areas, or with new structures and patterns in growing edges or in new areas. These changes over time have been discussed particularly well by ELISABETH LICHTENBERGER (1986), especially in her studies of Vienna, and by PETER SCHÖLLER in his monograph on German cities (1967).

As the urban population increases, cities expand outward, extending the outer boundaries, pushing the concentric rings farther from the center, thrusting the sectors farther afield, putting pressure on the boundaries between multiple nuclei. With growth there may be increasing traffic congestion in the city center with resulting centrifugal pressures. If political boundaries are frozen, as is typical in American cities, central cities lose population and separate suburban political units increase dramatically in population, function, and political power. Metropolitan areas rather than political cities increasingly are the focus of life and of scholarly studies. Networks of cities may become more dense.

Both the internal and external patterning of cities evolve over time. Changes reflect many factors: mere increase in population or density; evolving technology, particularly in transportation, shifting cultural, social, political, and economic contexts; evolving attitudes; and alterations in the level and type of security. These evolving patterns are complex and differ from one cultural realm to another.

I shall illustrate them by changes in transportation in American cities.

Evolving and new technologies in transportation transform areal relations internally within cities. The scale of spatial relations is altered by the change from movement on foot, to movement on horses or in horse-drawn carriages or wagons, or by electric tramways or streetcars, by gasoline or diesel-driven private cars, buses, and trucks, by suburban commuting trains, by construction of underground railways, by building of express highways, by airports, or by new communication linkages.

In North America the rise and overwhelming contemporary dominance of the automobile, together with congestion in inner parts of cities, has given rise, to the new urban form, the regional shopping center or shopping mall, with vast parking spaces for cars and with clusters of department stores and shops. These are located in suburban areas near large residential population. In the Chicago Metropolitan Area, these regional shopping centers typically are built between the older radial arteries in the formerly undeveloped interstices, which offer large blocks of land; they are located at or near the intersections of major newer expressways.

With the construction of the interstate highway system and peripheral freeways around the larger cities, suburban sites with good transport accessibility and large blocks of undeveloped land also become favorable sites for horizontal factories with immense parking lots for the automobiles of workers. The industrial structures may be clean, attractive, and surrounded by landscaped grounds. Los Angeles is a symbol of the automobile-dominated urbanized area with crisscrossing expressways, dispersed shopping malls, scattered high-rise office centers, and large industrial tracts. Los Angeles is notable for the weak development of a Central Business District and the absence of any form of mass transportation.

In Chicago a cross-commuting pattern has developed, with very heavy automobile traffic on radial highways in both directions, of industrial workers outward and of white-collar employees inward in the morning rush hour, and the

44

reverse in the evening rush hour, but with heavy automobile traffic throughout the day. This pattern reflects suburbanization of much retail trade and many factories, growth in the Central Business District of financial and office functions, suburban residences of white-collar employees and managers who work in the central city, and inner city residences of industrial workers, particularly of minority groups, who work in the suburbs.

Changing transportation has also affected external patterns of networks of cities. One recalls shifts in the relative importance of transport by wagons over unpaved roads, by ships on rivers, by barges on canals, by railroads, by express highways, and by air for specialty goods, services, and parts. With the increasing conquest of the space friction of distance and an increase in mobility of the population individuals are able conveniently to travel much longer distances. In North America this has resulted in the continuing decline or disappearance of smaller central places since early in the 20th century and in the relative increase in significance of the higher-order central places. Three factors have been involved in this change: better transportation, decrease in rural population with mechanization of agriculture, and increasing size of commercial establishments.

The interstate highway system in the United States with overnight truck deliveries among many cities has affected locational patterns for many industries. In the United States deregulation of airlines has put greater emphasis on metropolitan hubs with frequent and competitive service to other metropolitan hubs.

A few other contemporary innovations that are presently in process of transforming areal patterns of cities in the United States may be mentioned. ALLAN PRED (1977) has studied information circulation as a factor in the urban network of the United States and has noted the role of office activities, services, and quality of life in possible future developments. Television homogenizes the country and reduces urban-rural differences. Even the most remote homes in the United States with satellite dishes now have access to a large variety of television programs. With computers, word processors, and instantaneous telecommunication, many highly skilled professional activities are liberated from space contingencies for production. Thus both consumer-oriented services, as symbolized by television, and producer-oriented activities, as symbolized by the professional with a computer, are increasingly liberated from the necessities of particular locations. Silicon Valley is a symbol of this new age. Many activities are becoming increasing footloose not tied to physical proximity to particular centers, resources, or markets. In some cases the place of work and residence, long separated, are coming together again. The relative role of amenities as a location factor, as predicted by EDWARD L. ULLMAN (1954), has increased dramatically.

Evolving attitudes also play a role in patterns of urban land use. A good example is the increasing sensitivity of the population to land uses that are considered undesirable. Factories that produce high levels of air or water pollution are increasingly being expelled from central city loctions or densely populated areas. Activities that involve great hazards, such as nuclear power plants, are subject to increasingly stiff legal restrictions on location. The misguided early Soviet policy of locating nuclear power plants near the market nodes in metropolitan areas with inadequate safeguards was subject to the shock of the Chernobyl accident. In the United States no new nuclear power plants have been started for many years and some plants already under construction near major urban centers have been stopped. A whole new field of the study of natural and man-made hazards has arisen.

Cross-Cultural Perspectives

We now turn from historical evolution over time to cultural differences over space.

The typical residential unit illustrates profound national differences. As a result of personal preferences, long-standing traditions, public policies, and practices of financial institutions, the dominant American dwelling is a free-standing individual house surrounded by as much space as possible on all sides. The typical British dwelling is a row or semidetached house with a small front or back garden. The Japanese residence is a single house fully occupying a tiny lot but sometimes with a small internal garden. The Soviet housing unit is part of a multistory apartment in a large block development. These different housing types profoundly affect density of population, internal patterns of residential differentiation, and the type of transportation.

Americans seem to feel claustrophobia in small spaces. In lower quality dense apartments near the city center, life spills out into the street. In contrast the Japanese feel comfortable in small spaces, which they utilize with great efficiency, often using a single room successively during the day as bedroom, as living room, and as dining room. Thus population densities in Japan reach astonishingly high levels even in areas of single-family houses.

In American cities residential quality increases outward as higher income individuals opt for more spacious grounds. In some Asian cities, notably in Tokyo, Japan, residential locations near the center are eagerly sought because of ease of access to employment, recreation, and cultural activities. Homes in such central areas are beyond the economic means of most. I recall having been invited into the home of a young Japanese colleague in a central location in Tokyo. I asked how he could possibly afford a home in an area of such high land values and he replied that the site had been in his family for several generations. That is truly making use of one's ancestors.

The Harris-Ullman models of city patterns, both internal and external, were built on twentieth century conditions, particularly in American cities. They need modifications for the cities of Europe, where the structure of cities arose much earlier and historical buildings in some instances have served a sequence of diverse functions at different periods. These models may need greater modification when one crosses into other cultural realms. I will make a few comments based mainly on Soviet cities.

The contrasts between Soviet and American cities are enormous. Transport and housing symbolize the differences. The private automobile is dominant in American transportation while it is a negligible factor in the Soviet Union. Except in the largest metropolitan areas privately owned individual homes are the typical American dwelling. In Soviet cities individual houses or privately owned homes generally have been prohibited by law.

Governmental goals, policies, regulations, and practices all play a role in urban patterns in the Soviet Union. In the period of Communist government the urban population of the country increased from 20 million in 1920 to 190 million in 1990. Urban expansion during the Soviet period has had to accommodate 170 million new urban dwellers. Urban construction during the Soviet period accounts for nearly nine-tenths of the urban housing stock. No other such large area in the world has been under such centralized direction for such an extended period of rapid urban expansion. The urban plans are often idealistic verging on the utopian. But because of limited investment of funds and conflicts among different agencies, housing and community infrastructure often are deficient by Western standards. As JAMES BATER of Canada (1980) has demonstrated the ideal and the reality are far apart.

We turn first to the external patterns of distribution of cities in the Soviet Union.

Areal patterns of spacing of cities are associated roughly with the functions the cities serve. Cities with administrative, trade, and service functions tend to have a central-place distribution of even spacing over the territory with wider spacing of the cities with higher ranks in the hierarchy. Cities with transport functions display a linear pattern along railroad lines. Cities dominated by manufacturing often occur in cluster patterns.

The larger cities of the Soviet Union perform important administrative functions, which display a central-place distribution. The idea of hierarchy is deeply ingrained in Soviet communist doctrine. As the Soviet Russian poet MAIAKOVSKII expressed it in Russian: „Nachinaetsia zemlia, kak izvestno, ot kremlia," or in English, "The country begins, as is well known, at the kremlin." This has been true both historically and in present-day organizsation. Or as N. N. BARANSKII, the Soviet economic geographer, put it, "Cities are like the command staff of a country organizing it in all its relations, economic, political-administrative, and cultural. As in a command staff, cities have their hierarchy."

Rank size analysis (HARRIS 1970) confirms the concordance of politically determined regional centers with city-size distributions. But the urban network of this vast sprawling territory is not completely integrated. Outlying regions separated by culture, as in the Baltics, the Caucasus, or Middle Asia, or by distance as Siberia or the Far East do not depend on Moscow for all of the highest-order services in the central-place hierarchy in spite of the highly centralized directing communist party and the command economy that have characterized the Soviet state during most of its history. Indeed the struggle between primacy of Moscow and greater autonomy for regional centers is one of the most sensitive and important current policy issues in the Soviet Union.

Much has been written in the Soviet literature about a unified settlement system (Khorev 1979) but actual measures to implement such a system appear to be lacking.

Transportation is required to tie the vast Soviet Union together. It is not surprising, therefore, to find linear alignment of cities along transport routes. Most striking is the line of transport centers distributed like beads on a string along the Trans-Siberian Railroad.

In the Soviet Union clustering patterns are characteristic for many raw-material oriented industrial cities that mushroomed during the Stalin period, most notably in the Donets Basin and the Kuznetsk Basin. The Soviet literature is extensive on the concept of territorial production complexes but actual measures to implement this concept are hard to find.

Because of centralized policies of emphasis on physical production, manufacturing industries play a larger role in Soviet cities than in either post-industrial cities of advanced countries in Western Europe, North America, Japan, or Australia, where the tertiary and quaternary activities have become relatively more important, or in the cities of the Third World, still largely in the preindustrial phase of development. It may be noted also that specialized manufacturing cities in the Soviet Union tend to be raw-material-oriented in contrast to the United States where they are more often oriented towards the market (Harris 1954).

We turn now to internal patterns. The study of internal patterns of Soviet cities has been seriously impeded by several factors. First of all, statistics generally are not available for internal parts of cities, that is for blocks, communities, or districts. Secondly, appropriate large-scale base maps are not available to scholars or the public. I recall once hearing a lecture in the Moscow Branch of the Geographical Society of the USSR on the urban patterns of Moscow. The only map displayed was an extremely crude touristic sketch. Detailed accurate maps long have been considered state secrets for fear that they might be used by a foreign enemy. Third, field work generally has been impeded, at least for foreigners. Studies of actual internal patterns of Soviet cities, as distinct from generalized idealized plans, generally have not been on the official research programs of Soviet investigators. These conditions are changing but the legacy of the past lays a heavy hand on the present. Our statement on internal patterns are therefore somewhat general and impressionistic.

Presumably in the Soviet Union the quality of housing in cities does not differ as much as in American cities. Housing-construction policies have favored the development of huge tracts of homogeneous housing. In some socialist cities, however, inner locations may be preferred, especially for greater accessibility and the saving of time and effort in transportation required for long-distance commuting. In some socialist cities there is a preference for the older presocialist housing near the center to the new standardized blocks of flats farther out. In Warsaw housing near the center is reported to be especially prized (DANGSCHAT 1985).

Over-all population densities are reported to decrease very steeply outward in Moscow but the areal units for reporting data are so large that interpretations are difficult. Population densities are very high and may increase outward in some sectors as one moves from older presocialist housing near the center to great blocks of new socialist high-rise high-density apartments built on available land farther out. Population densities also exhibit differences by sectors, A map of population density by 29 districts of Moscow reveals four sectors of high density, four of medium density, and one of low density in central Moscow (LAPPO et al 1976, p. 93).

These examples demonstrate the need for detailed studies of individual cities. They also emphasize the importance of careful ordering of the data to reveal the underlying patterns.

OLGA MEDVEDKOV, formerly of the Soviet Union but now of the United States (1990) has revealed the very weak development of the service sector in Soviet cities. Indeed she concludes that many of the Soviet cities have the characteristics of company towns, that is towns whose infrastructure is weak and is determined by and oriented toward the industrial establishments. The service sector in the economy in the Soviet Union occupies only a half to a third as high a proportion of the employed persons in the population as in Western Cities. The Central Business District is relatively inconspicuous in the landscape.

Soviet cities reveal the modest provision of housing space per capita, as government investment has been directed toward industrial construction. Much of the housing has actually been constructed by factories or other establishments for the workers and employees. These separate blocks of associated employment and housing have some of the characteristics of multiple nuclei settlements. The widely dispersed units of the city of Bratsk offer an example.

Soviet cities display differentiation by sectors. Perhaps the most widely known example is the scientific-educational sector of Moscow in October District extending from the central city south-southwest along Leninskiy Prospekt past the Academy of Sciences and its many research institutes to Lenin Hills and Moscow State University. Nearly all the homes of Soviet colleagues I have visited lie in this sector. Both residential and industrial satellite cities have developed by sectors aligned along the major radiating railroad lines.

Soviet housing generally has been built on the neighborhood principle of internal access within communities to schools, playgrounds, shops, and community facilities, a principle less well developed in Western capitalistic or welfare-state conditions where there are many actors in urban development.

49

Geographisches Institut
der Universität Kiel
Neue Universität

Some Soviet cities display a linear pattern. Volgograd along the Volga River and Magnitogorsk aligned along the iron and steel works are examples.

Within the Soviet Union the rich diversity of ethnic groups, or nationalities, within cities offers a promising field for comparative studies. About half the cities form a core of ethnically homogeneous cities in Russia proper (the R.S.F.S.R.). Broad bands of cities on the western and southern borders of the Soviet Union, however, consist of ethnically complex cities with varying proportions of a regional nationality, often the basis of a non-Russian union republic, notably in the Baltic region, in the Caucasus, and in Soviet Middle Asia (HARRIS 1945).

A special urban pattern has been developed where two civilizations are in contact. A European city and an Asian may exist side by side. Such cities in Soviet Middle Asia have been well described, particularly by German scholars: ERNST GIESE, WILHELM MÜLLER-WILLE, and JOHANNES F. GELLERT. Tashkent and Samarkand have radically different adjacent sectors occupied by Russian officials and Uzbek inhabitants. I recall a visit to a home of an Uzbek colleague in Tashkent. He was an important scientist, a member of the Uzbek Academy of Sciences, and head of a major research institute. He explained to me that although the Academy of Sciences had built modern Soviet-style housing for the personnel of his Institute, only the Russians lived there. He and other Uzbeks of his institute preferred to live in the Uzbek quarter. He himself had built his own house of adobe brick surrounded by tall trees and an irrigated vegetable garden and a fruit orchard. This provided him and his family with privacy, the dignity of independence, and fresh fruit and vegetables.

It is specifically because of these cultural differences that are reflected in both the internal and external patterning of cities that I welcome this symposium on Modelling the City: Cross-Cultural Perspectives.

Bibliography:

BATER, JAMES H. The Soviet City: Ideal and Reality. London: Edward Arnold; New York: Holmes & Meier, 1980. 196 p.

BEAUJEU-GARNIER, JACQUELINE. Géographie urbaine. Paris: Armand Colin, 1980. 360 p.

BERRY, BRIAN J. L., and PARR, JOHN B., with others. Market Centers and Retail Location: Theory and Applications. Englewood Cliffs, New Jersey; London: Prentice-Hall, 1988.

BERRY, BRIAN J. L., and HARRIS, CHAUNCY D. Central Places. International Encyclopedia of the Social Sciences. New York: Macmillan and the Free Press, 1968, vol. 2, pp. 365–370.

BÖHM, HANS. Soziale und räumliche Organisation der Stadt. Vorstellungen in der geographischen, städtebaulichen und nationalökonomischen Literatur Deutschlands vor 1918. Colloquium Geographicum. Band 19. Beiträge zur empirischen Wirtschaftsgeographie. Festschrift Helmut Hahn zum 65. Geburtstag, 1986, pp. 33–55.

CHRISTALLER, WALTER. Die zentralen Orte in Süddeutschland: Eine ökonomisch-geographische Untersuchung über die Gesetzmäßigkeit der Verbreitung und Entwicklung der Siedlungen mit städtischen Funktionen. Jena: Verlag von Gustav Fischer, 1933. 331 p. Reprinted [2nd ed.]: Darmstadt: Wissenschaftliche Buchgesellschaft, 1968. 331 p. 3rd ed., 1980. 340 p.

CHRISTALLER, WALTER. Central Places in Southern Germany. Translated by Carlisle W. Baskin. Englewood Cliffs. New Jersey: Prentice Hall, 1966. 230 p.

DANGSCHAT, JENS. Soziale und räumliche Ungleichheit in Warschau. Hamburg: Hans Christians Verlag, 1985. 259 p. Beiträge zur Stadtforschung, Band 10.

FRENCH, R. A. The Individuality of the Soviet City, in R. A. FRENCH and F. E. IAN HAMILTON, eds. The Socialist City, pp. 73–104.

FRENCH, R. A. and HAMILTON, F. E. IAN, editors. The Socialist City: Spatial Structure and Urban Policy. Chichester, England; New York: John Wiley, 1979. 541 p.

GELLERT, JOHANNES F., and ENGELMANN, GERHARD. Entwicklung und Struktur einiger sowjetischer Großstädte in Mittelasien, Geographische Berichte, Band 12, no. 44 (1967, no. 3), pp. 175–203.

GIESE, E. Aufbau, Entwicklung und Genese der islamisch-orientalischen Stadt in Sowjet-Mittelasien. Erdkunde, Band 34 (1980), pp. 46–60.

GORMSEN, ERDMANN, editor. Periodische Märkte in verschiedenen Kulturkreisen. Vorträge der Fachsitzung 15 des 42. Deutschen Geographentages Göttingen 1979. Periodic Markets in Different Cultural Realms. Papers Presented at Session 15 of the 42nd Conference of German Geographers, Göttingen 1979. Mainzer Geographische Studien, Heft 21, 1982. 82 p.

GORMSEN, ERDMANN, and SMITH, ROBERT H. T., editors. Market-Place Exchange: Empirical and Theoretical Studies. Papers Presented at the Meeting of the International Geographical Union Working Group on Market-Place Exchange Systems, Nagoya, Japan, August 1980. Mainzer Geographische Studien, Heft 24, 1982. 104 p.

HAMILTON, F. E. IAN. The Moscow City Region. Oxford: Oxford University Press, 1976. 48 p. Problem Regions of Europe.

HARRIS, CHAUNCY D. A Functional Classification of Cities in the United States, Geographical Review, vol.33, no. 1 (January 1943), pp. 86–99.

HARRIS, CHAUNCY D. Suburbs, American Journal of Sociology, vol. 49, no. 1 (July 1943), pp. 1–13.

HARRIS, CHAUNCY D. Cities of the Soviet Union, Geographical Review, vol. 35, no. 1 (January 1945), pp. 107–121.

HARRIS, CHAUNCY D. Ethnic Groups in Cities of the Soviet Union, Geographical Review, vol. 35, no. 3 (July 1945), pp. 466–473.

HARRIS, CHAUNCY D. The Market as a Factor in the Localisation of Industry in the United States, Annals of the Association of American Geographers, vol. 44, no. 4 (December 1954), pp. 283–299.

HARRIS, CHAUNCY D. Cities of the Soviet Union: Studies in Their Functions, Size, Density, and Growth. Chicago: Rand McNally, 1970. 484 p. Association of American Geographers. Monograph Series, vol. 5. 2nd printing. Washingthon D.C.: Association of American Geographers, 1972.

HARRIS, CHAUNCY D. Les Révolutions urbaine et démographique et l'accroissement de la population urbaine en Union Soviétique. Bulletin de l'Association de Géographes Francais, no. 385–386 (janvier-février 1971), pp. 17–32.

HARRIS, CHAUNCY D. The Urban and Industrial Transformation of Japan. Geographical Review, vol. 72, no. 1 (January 1982), pp. 50–89.

HARRIS, CHAUNCY D., and ULLMAN, EDWARD L. The Nature of Cities. Annals of the American Academy of Political and Social Science, vol. 242 (November 1945), pp. 7–17.

HOFMEISTER, BURKHARD. Stadt und Kulturraum Angloamerika. Braunschweig: Friedr. Vieweg + Sohn, 1971. 341 p.

HOFMEISTER, BURKHARD. Stadtgeographie. 4th ed. Braunschweig: Georg Westermann Verlag, 1980. 200 p. Das Geographische Seminar.

HOFMEISTER, BURKHARD. Die Stadtstruktur: Ihre Ausprägung in den verschiedenen Kulturräumen der Erde. Darmstadt: Wissenschaftliche Buchgesellschaft, 1980. 201 p.

KHOREV, B. S. Gorodskie poseleniia SSSR (Problemy rosta i ikh izuchenie): Ocherki geografii rasseleniia. Moscow: "Mysl'" 1968. 254 p.

KHOREV, B. S. Problemy gorodov [vol. 2] (Ekonomiko-geograficheskoe issledovanie gorodskogo rasseleniia v SSSR). Moscow: "Mysl'," 1971. 413 p.

KHOREV, B. S. Problemy gorodov (Urbanizatsiia i edinaia sistema rasseleniia v SSSR). 2nd ed. Moscow: "Mysl'," 1975. 428 p.

LAPPO, G. M. Goroda na puti v budushchee. Moscow: "Mysl'," 1987. 236 p.

LAPPO, G., CHIKISHEV, A., and BEKKER, A. Moscow: Capital of the Soviet Union. Moscow: Progress Publishers, 1976. 189 p.

LICHTENBERGER, ELISABETH. Stadtgeographie. Band 1. Begriffe, Konzepte, Modelle, Prozesse. Stuttgart: B. G. Teubner, 1986. 280 p. Teubner Studienbücher der Geographie.

MEDVEDKOW, OLGA. Soviet Urbanization. London; New York: Routledge, 1990. 168 p.

MULLER, PETER O. Contemporary Suburban America. Englewood Cliffs, New Jersey: Prentice Hall, 1981. 218 p.

MÜLLER-WILLE, WILHELM. Stadt und Umland im südlichen Sowjet-Mittelasien. Wiesbaden: Franz Steiner, 1978, 48 p. Erdkundliches Wissen, Heft 49.

PALLOT, JUDITH, and SHAW, DENIS J. B. Planning in the Soviet Union. London: Croom Helm; Athens, Georgia: University of Georgia Press, 1981. 303 p.

PALM, RISA. The Geography of American Cities. New York; Oxford: Oxford University Press, 1981. 365 p.

PRED, ALLAN. City-Systems in Advanced Economies: Past Growth, Present Processes and Future Development Options. London: Hutchinson; New York: John Wiley, 1977. 256 p.

SAUSHKIN, IU. G., and GALUSHKOVA, V. G. Moskva sredy gorodov mira: Ekonomiko-geograficheskoe issledovanie. Moscow: "Mysl'," 1983. 285 p.

SCHÖLLER, PETER. Die deutschen Städte. Wiesbaden: Franz Steiner Verlag, 1967. Erdkundliches Wissen, Heft 17. 107 p.

SMITH, ROBERT H. T., editor. Market-place Trade: Periodic Markets, Hawkers, and Traders in Africa, Asia, and Latin America. Vancouver BC: Center for Transportation Studies, 1978. 264 p.

SMITH, ROBERT H. T., and GORMSEN, ERDMANN, editors. Market-Place Exchange: Spatial Analysis and Policy. Papers presented at the Meeting of the International Geographical Union Working Group on Market-Place Systems, Zaria, Nigeria, July 1978. Mainzer Geographische Studien, Heft 17. 1979. 136 p.

ULLMAN, EDWARD L. Amenities as a Factor in Regional Growth. The Geographical Review, vol. 44, no. 1 (January 1954), pp. 119–132.

ULLMAN, EDWARD L. The Nature of Cities Reconsidered. The Regional Science Association, Papers and Proceedings, vol. 9 (1962), pp. 7–23.

YEATES, MAURICE, and GARNER, BARRY. The North American City. 3rd ed. New York: Harper and Row, 1980. 558 p.

THE NORTH AMERICAN CITY

With 6 figures

BURKHARD HOFMEISTER

1. The North American city as a distinct cultural-genetic type

There are three levels of research in the investigation of urban structures. Let us first look at the extreme positions. The microlevel is represented by the *individual city* with its unique site, origin and historical development and its peculiar mixture of urban functions and land uses. HARRIS and ULLMAN in their famous paper on "The nature of cities" of 1945 characterized this idiographic point of view with the following statement: ,Each city is unique in detail but resembles others in function and pattern'.

At the macrolevel the cities of the entire world are reviewed on the basis of features all of them have in common: the city is considered *a type of settlement of global distribution* exposing certain forms and functions that make it a city.

Both points of view, the individual level as well as the global level, may be successfully applied to urban geography. Both points of view may have their merits in detecting the nature of cities. However, even by making both approaches, the geographer will not be able to do full justice to the complexity of urban phenomena.

Somewhere between the two extremes there is an intermediate level by means of which it is possible to look at a *group of cities in a particular region* of the world exposing a limited number of features making them resemble each other, but, at the same time, making them look different from the cities in other regions. These features may originate in ideas and thoughts of their inhabitants and the desire of people to create their settlements accordingly. Cities are, to a certain degree, a mirror of the intentions of their founding fathers and successive generations of residents.

The somewhat indifferent term ,region' was applied on purpose in want of some further consideration. Similarities on the one hand and differences on the other hand vary according to the *degree of abstraction* chosen for any particular investigation. If we consider the North American city a distinct regional type of urban settlement, we have got to beware of the fact that we have chosen the highest possible degree of abstraction, i.e. the *culture realm* or Kulturerdteil in terms of ALBERT KOLB'S understanding. It ist this cultural-genetic type of city that will be the object of the present paper.

To be sure, we do neglect all the regional variations that may be found within the huge North American culture realm. As GOLDBERG and MERCER in their book ,The myth of the North American city: continentalism challenged' pointed out the international boundary between the United States that became a sovereign state in 1776 and Canada that before acquiring its dominion status in 1867 had been British North America under British rule made for considerable differences between such cities as Chicago and Toronto. Thus, while applying a lower degree of abstraction, one may very well distinguish between the Canadian city on the one hand and the U.S. city on the other hand.

A further differentiation by ALFRED HECHT led to the distinction between the Anglophone city and the Francophone city in Canada. In the same manner one may distinguish between the cities of the colonial period in the English, French and Spanish spheres of influence in the present-day United States and the cities founded during the westward expansion of the United States during the nineteenth century in the vast region surveyed according to the Land Ordinance of 1785. It is mainly this region that we refer to while speaking of the North American City as a cultural-genetic type.

2. Dominant structural features of the North American city

I shall limit myself to five important features of North American urban structure: the Central Business District (CBD), the zone of transition , the inner residential quarters, the sectors of special development, and suburbia.

The core of the city has, usually on the basis of a *grid pattern,* developed as the *Central Business District.* This very term now widely used in urban geography all over the world was created in the United States and derived from the North American prototype. It therefore proved not easily transferable to different culture realms. For the threshold set for the so-called CBD intensity index is based on the usually very intensive commercial uses of the central blocks and the almost entire expulsion of any residential use, or, in other words, an extremely high degree of functional segregation. The threshold set for the CBD height index is based on the great local *concentration of skyscrapers* with their immense amounts of retail and office space. Both features have reached extreme dimensions in North American cities and are hardly found outside the North American culture realm.

The CBD's circumference is the so-called *zone of transition* with its auxiliary functions for the CBD such as wholesaling, warehousing and transportation enterprises and particular commercial uses such as printing, functions that have been expelled from the CBD proper by virtue of its extremely high rental rates. The transition zone is a very dynamic urban area with CBD functions progressing into its better portions and with central functions of a high order retreating from its less favourable portions.

The *inner residential quarters* surrounding the transition zone are characterized by a decaying building stock, this being at least partly due to the fact that many houses had been constructed of wood and are prone to rather quick deterioration. These quarters are further characterized by so-called red-lining, i.e. financial institutions refuse to grant mortgages to home owners in such areas, also by frequent tax delinquencies and vacancies. Measures taken against such negative developments are, above all, urban renewal on the basis of federal subsidies and urban homesteading by the respective communities that transfer tax delinquent and vacant homes to families of low income who are willing to restore the house mainly with the family labour force. In some cities gentrification has made for the upgrading of inner residential quarters. This is also the zone of the often large minority ghettoes including the so-called black belts, the residential areas of the black population. The latter are lacking a counterpart in the Canadian cities.

There are usually *two sectoral developments* to be observed in the North American city. There is, on the one hand, a certain sectoral *outward movement of social-status groups* from their inner residential areas to adjoining suburban residential areas. On the other hand, there are *wedges of manufacturing plants* along railway lines reaching right to the limits of the CBD. This phenomenon is a result of the fact that in the vast area west of the Appalachian Mountains the plotting of towns and the construction of railways usually occurred simultaneously. In many cases the railway companies were the very founders of towns. The town was thus centered around the railway station, while the tracks were cutting through the town center and attracting manufactures to the premises right outside the core that was eventually to become the CBD.

The *ring of the outer suburbs* is no longer exclusively dominated by the detached single-family home. However, for several decades high income levels, favourable conditions of developers for prospective home owners, relatively low real estate prices due to the use of timber as the dominant building material, the high degree of private car ownership, and the extensive construction of urban expressways were *conducive to urban sprawl*. Special mention should be made of the mobile home courts that had been banished to the areas beyond the city limits by the zoning laws of many cities.

The construction of dwelling units was followed or, in quite a few cases, even preceded by the suburbanization of retail trade and services in modern *shopping centers* and the suburbanization of industrial workplaces. The period of the founding of large numbers of *industrial parks* was followed, since about 1965, by the founding of office parks or *business parks*. In many cases such business parks were expansions of already existing shopping centers, thus creating what has been termed an *urban village*. Urban villages – this term being a contradictio in adjecto – are characterized by their medium densities of population which is somewhat lower than that of the inner residential quarters and at the same time somewhat higher than that of the single-family housing suburbs, thus guaranteeing a minimum number of residents required for the maintenance of certain cultural amenities. Particularly favourable locations are the exits of urban expressways and especially the intersections of a perimeter expressway and a radial urban expressway.

This polynuclear development of a great number of clusters has brought about a *high degree of fragmentation* of the metropolitan areas. I cannot agree, however, with Lutz Holzner's ‚Stadtland USA' concept and his statement that there are no longer cities in the traditional sense of the word in the United States, and that cities as compact urban places belong to the past and don't exist any more.

3. Urban structure as reflected in selected models

The early models of urban structure by Hurd 1903, by Burgess 1925, by Hoyt 1939 and by Harris/Ullman 1945 were developed in the United States, but will not be treated here in any detail. I shall limit myself to models presented by various authors during the last three decades.

Boskoff (1962) in his book "The sociology of urban regions" presented what he called 'a simplified diagram of the urban region' (Fig. 1). He distinguished between the central city, the suburban zone with residential and industrial suburbs, the urban fringe, satellite cities and exurbia. We can easily detect zonal and polynuclear elements in his model, whereas sectoral elements are lacking. Boskoff in his written text draws on examples from *various parts of the world* so that his diagram, although it does reflect metropolitan development in the United States to a certain degree, should not stricly be labelled a model of the North American city.

Before presenting models of the early 1970s I should like to turn to two models of the year 1979 since these are *partial models* reflecting certain aspects of urban structure only.

The model presented by Rees in his investigation of Chicago in 1979 (Fig. 2) is a model based on *residential choice*. Burgess in 1925 postulated the outward expansion of his various zones, Rees anticipates the constant addition of new housing in the periphery. This constant offer of new residences meets responses by each of the social classes at the periphery of their respective residential areas. ‚There is an out-movement from older housing areas to newer housing areas in each sector on the part of the upwardly mobile in the "not well-off" sector and on the part of the space and family oriented households in the "well-off" sector' (Rees 1979, p. 159). Thus the zonal structure based on the age of building stock is superimposed by a sectoral movement of residents on the basis of social status.

Watson presented a model derived from *land values* in his books of 1979 "Social geography of the United States" and of 1982 "The United States: habitation of hope". His 1979 graph (Fig. 3) also contains a curve of land values, whereas his 1982 presentation is a dynamic model of six stages of development. Since the latter model is also based on land values, reference here is only made to the former model of 1979.

In the Festschrift in honour of Walter Gerling published in 1972 Holzner presented a model that has been considered outdated by the author in his more

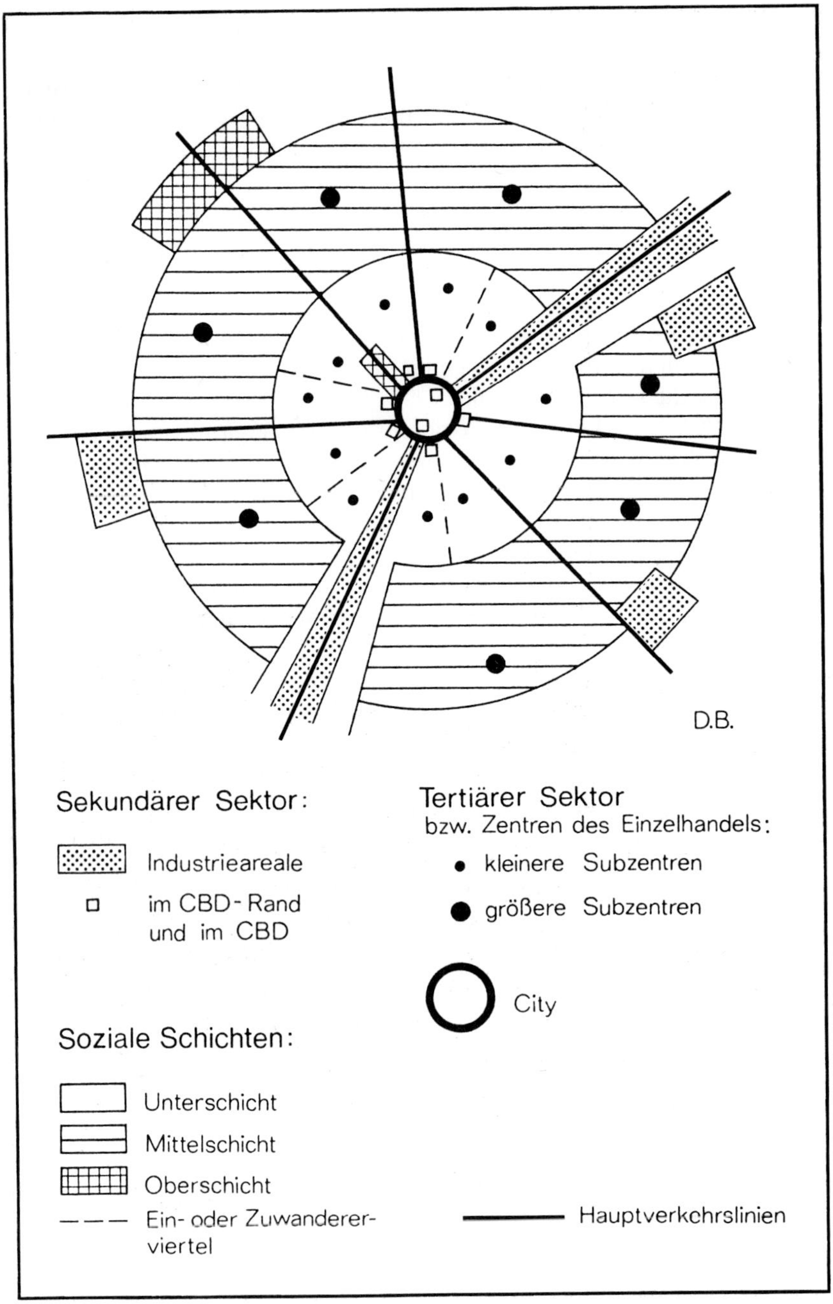
D.B.
Sekundärer Sektor:
Industrieareale
im CBD-Rand und im CBD
Tertiärer Sektor bzw. Zentren des Einzelhandels:
kleinere Subzentren
größere Subzentren
City
Soziale Schichten:
Unterschicht
Mittelschicht
Oberschicht
Ein- oder Zuwanderer-viertel
Hauptverkehrslinien

Fig. 1: The urban region (after BOSKOFF 1962)

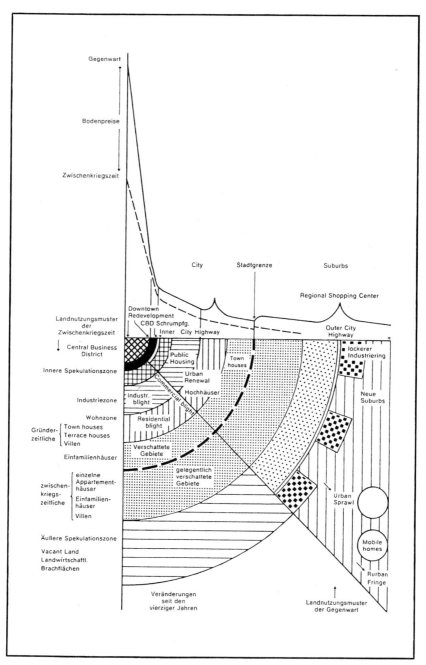

Fig. 2: The integrated ring and sector model of American cities (after REES 1969)

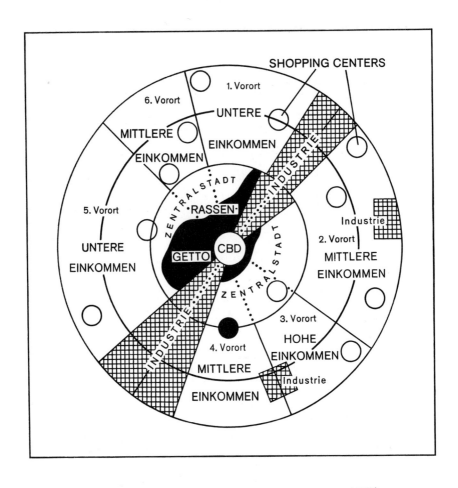

Fig. 3: The model of an American city (after Watson 1979)

recent publications, but that nevertheless proves to be very useful, for in my opinion it is *highly realistic* due to the following advantages (Fig. 4):

Firstly, it reflects zonal as well as sectoral and polynuclear elements of the North American city;

Secondly, the ghettoes of minority groups in the inner residential areas including the black belt are explicitly presented;

Thirdly, the sectoral elements of residential areas of various social groups as well as of industrial zones along transportation arteries are shown;

Fourthly, shopping centers and industrial parks represent the polynuclear element and give credit to the high degree of fragmentation of the metropolitan area.

60

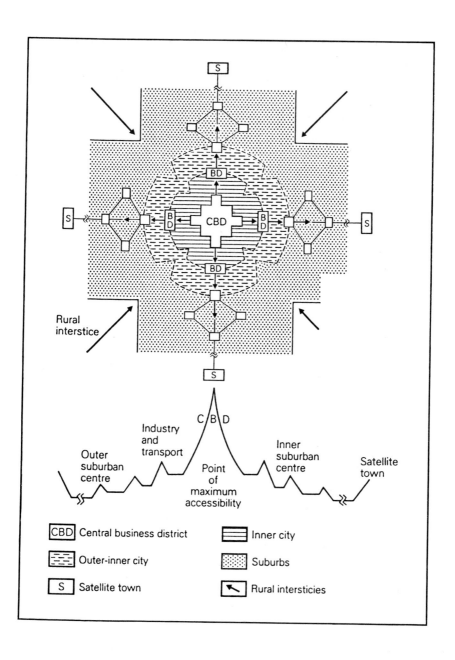

Fig. 4: Model of the U.S. city (after Holzner 1972)

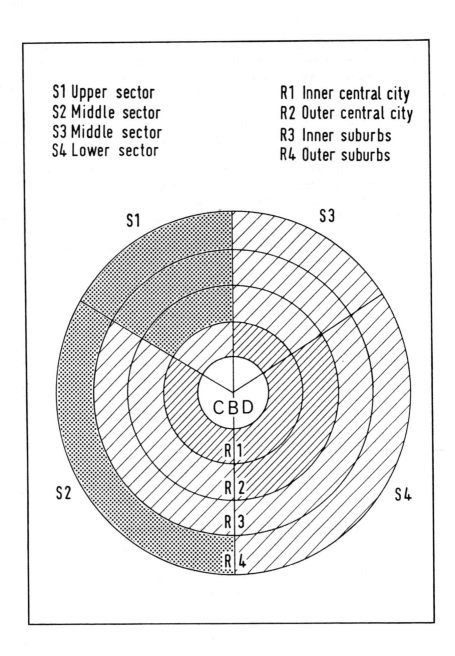

Fig. 5: Development of Metropolitan Areas in the U.S. Northeast since the interwar era (after Lichtenberger 1975)

In addition to Holzner's model of 1972 two more models shall be briefly reviewed. Lichtenberger's 'Development of metropolitan areas of the U.S. Northeast since the interwar area' of 1975 (Fig. 5) goes much more into details as to the *various processes* of housing construction and changes of land use. On the other hand, a differentiation of residential quarters of various social groups can only be indirectly deduced from the mosaic of land uses shown in the model. In a sense, Lichtenberg's model is a further elaboration of, and a good supplement to, the Holzner model of 1972.

Finally Stewig's model of 1983 (Fig. 6) has been selected for this comparative overview. Stewig explicitly draws on Holzner, but goes more into details as far as *intraurban location* of manufacturing and the intraurban hierarchy of shopping centers are concerned. On the other hand, his presentation of residential areas is

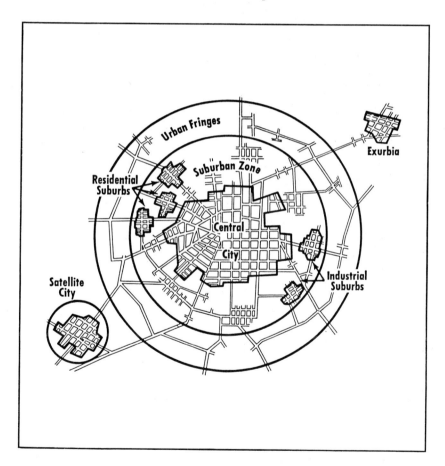

Fig. 6: Model of the North American city (after Stewig 1983

63

too vague and suggests a *social gradient* from the urban periphery to the city center throughout the entire metropolitan area that is not so generally found in reality.

To sum up, there are certain elements of the structure of North American cities that had developed as early as the nineteenth century such as the railway corridors with the development of industrial sectors right outside the CBD, and there are other elements that have been added in much more recent times such as the numerous shopping centers, industrial parks, and business parks. These changes have usually been very profound and very rapid in North America, thus urging the geographer to constant revisions of his concepts and to constant changes of his perception and graphic presentation of the North American city.

References:

Boskoff, A.: The sociology of urban regions. New York 1962, second ed. 1970.

Burgess, E. W.: The growth of the city. In: Park, R. E./McKenzie, R. D./Burgess, E. (eds.) The city. Chicago 1925.

Goldberg, M. A./Mercer, J.: Canadian and U.S. cities: Basic differences, possible explanations, and their meaning for public policy. Pap. of the Region. Sci. Assoc. vol 45, p. 159−183.

Goldberg, M. A./Mercer, J.: The myth of the North American city: Continentalism challenged. Vancouver 1986.

Harris, C. D./Ullman, E. L.: The nature of cities. Ann. Amer. Acad. of. Polit. and Soc. Sci. 242, Nov. 1945.

Hecht, A.: Die anglo- und frankokanadische Stadt. Ein sozio-ökonomischer Vergleich am Beispiel von Hamilton and Quebec City. In: Niederehe, H.-J., Schroeder-Lanz, H. (eds.): Beiträge zur landeskundlich-linguistischen Kenntnis von Quebec. Trierer Geogr. Stud. Sonderh. 1. Trier 1977.

Hofmeister, B.: Stadt und Kulturraum: Angloamerika. Braunschweig 1971.

Holzner, L.: Sozialsegregation und Wohnviertelsbildung in amerikanischen Städten, dargestellt am Beispiel Milwaukee. In: Gerling-Festschrift. Würzburg 1972.

Holzner, L.: Stadtland USA – Zur Auflösung und Neuordnung der US-amerikanischen Stadt. Geogr. Zeitschr. 1985.

Hoyt, H.: The structure and growth of residential neighborhoods in American cities. Washington D.C. 1939.

Hurd, R. M.: City land values. New York 1903.

Kolb, A.: Die Geographie und die Kulturerdteile. In: Hermann v. Wißmann-Festschrift. Tübingen 1962, p. 42−49.

Kolb, A.: Die Pazifische Welt. Kultur- und Wirtschaftsräume am Stillen Ozean. Kleine Geogr. Schriften Bd. 3. Berlin 1981.

Lichtenberger, E.: Die Stadterneuerung in den USA. Ber. z. Raumordn. u. Raumforsch. 6, 1975, p. 3−16.

Rees, P. H.: Residential patterns in American cities: 1960. Univ. of. Chicago Dept. of Geogr. Res. Pap. 189. Chicago 1979.

Stewig, R.: Die Stadt in Industrie- und Entwicklungsländern. UTB 1247. Paderborn/München/Wien/Zürich 1983.

Watson, J. W.: Social geography of the United States. Longman Group UK. London 1979.

Watson, J. W.: The United States: Habitation of hope. London 1982.

THE LATIN AMERICAN CITY

With 4 figures and 3 tables

J. Bähr and G. Mertins

Each Latin American city has of course its own individual, unmistakable features, and we do also have certain regional city types that have gone through similar development phases and have similar functions (e.g., *frontera* cities in Amazonia and Gran Chaco or the cities of the central coffee zone of Colombia). Nevertheless, all of these cities have a number of patterns and structural characteristics in common.

Before we attempt to briefly describe these shared patterns we should, however, point out that the division of Latin America into a sphere dominated by Spanish language and culture and one dominated by Portuguese language and culture led to differences in urban morphology, structure and functions in the more important colonial cities (Wilhelmy and Borsdorf 1984, p. 22f.). The major cities of the Spaniards, the later capitals of various Latin American countries, were founded as the centers of Spanish military, political and ecclesiastical power. As such they were built primarily at sites that had been centers of Indian civilization (e.g., Mexico, Bogotá, Quito); i.e., the "continental" location was the most important locational factor for major Spanish colonial cities. The exceptions were a few harbors or inland base stations (e.g., Callao, Valparaiso, Cartagena, Mompós). The most important Portuguese cities, in contrast, originating as trading posts and bases for seafarers, grew up predominantly along the Atlantic coast. The locational factor "coast" or rather a location conducive to transport and trade) played a very important role in the regional economic development of the country up to the very recent past, e.g., in Brazil.

If we disregard this viewpoint and the conspicuous differences in the layout (Portuguese cities have no grid pattern) and take into account that the later changes in the colonial urban structure did not begin at the same time or take place with the same intensity, we find considerable similarities between the cities of Latin America in their historical and their present functional and sociospatial structure. The similarities are so extensive that we appear justified in speaking of the Latin American type of city, especially when we are making comparisons on a continental scale.

Already in the late 1970s and early 1980s we tried to summarize these similarities in a model of the social and functional structure of Latin American cities (Bähr and Mertins 1981 and earlier Bähr 1976, Mertins 1980). This model was based on an evaluation of a large number of investigations by other authors and by ourselves (on Bogotá, Quito, Lima and Santiago de Chile, above all). About the same time other German authors developed comparable models

(Gormsen 1981; Borsdorf 1976 for medium-sized Latin American cities). The basic tenor of these models is so similar that we need not discuss them in detail here (cf. Wilhelmy and Borsdorf 1984, p. 181ff for a summary).

For the following we shall proceed from the model we developed in 1981 (Fig. 1). If we interpret this model as a dynamic model of development over space and time and include intraurban migration in our analysis, we can comprehend it as a model of the spatiotemporal development of the Latin American city, i.e., it can serve to explain the developmental steps a town goes through prior to becoming a big city (small town, medium-sized town, cf. Mertins 1991).

The basic principles of the internal differentiation of Latin American cities form three different, partially overlapping patterns, which did not develop at the same time and with the same distinctness everywhere:

1. An older pattern of concentric rings in the city center, often dating back to the colonial period, but meanwhile modified to a greater or lesser extent. The original basis for this annular structure was the social gradient from the center to the periphery with the consequent decrease in the size of housing and the quality of the housing stock from the central plaza toward the urban fringe ("reverse" Burgess type). In the large cities it is evident today in a sequence that is almost exclusively functionally determined, a sequence running from the CBD, which usually developed in the old town center, via a mixed residential, commercial and industrial zone to the marginal inner-city districts (slums), which are usually scattered around in patches, however, rather than being arranged in rings. Contrarily, in most small towns we still encounter the traditional sociospatial pattern, whereas in the medium-sized towns it is already in the process of disintegration, albeit to varying degrees (cf. the example below of Manizales, Colombia).

2. A pattern characterized more strongly by wedge-like sectors in the Hoytian sense (1939), i.e., settlement and industrial expansion along growth axes, which began to develop in the big cities in the 1930s (even earlier in some cases). These were, for one thing, the outgrowth of increasing industrialization following the worldwide depression of the 1930s (not until after World War II in some countries). In the process large industrial complexes were established along these growth axes, with lower-class districts arising in their immediate vicinity, and along railroad lines and highways. Additionally, they are a result of the gradual out-migration of the upper classes, and later of the upper-middle and middle classes, out of the once highly prized districts around the central plaza and the gradual relocation of such districts into areas farther and farther from the town center, usually continuing outward in the direction they originally started in. To a lesser degree these processes can also be observed in medium-sized towns.

3. A cellular, discontinuous settlement structure at or ahead of the current periphery, which is extremely characteristic of the rapid, often unrestrained areal growth of the large cities since the 1960s and was caused by growing migration pressure. Three types of settlement are typically found in this peripheral area:

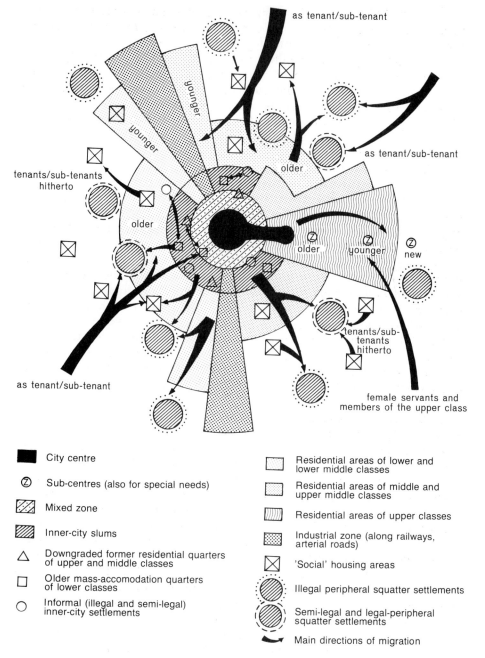

as tenant/sub-tenant

younger

younger

older

tenants/sub-tenants
hitherto

older

older younger new

tenants/sub-
tenants
hitherto

as tenant/sub-tenant

as tenant/sub-tenant

female servants and
members of the upper class

■ City centre		Residential areas of lower and lower middle classes
Ⓩ Sub-centres (also for special needs)		Residential areas of middle and upper middle classes
Mixed zone		Residential areas of upper classes
Inner-city slums		Industrial zone (along railways, arterial roads)
△ Downgraded former residential quarters of upper and middle classes		'Social' housing areas
□ Older mass-accomodation quarters of lower classes		Illegal peripheral squatter settlements
○ Informal (illegal and semi-legal) inner-city settlements		Semi-legal and legal-peripheral squatter settlements
		Main directions of migration

Fig. 1: Model of the Latin American city (Source: Bähr and Mertins 1981)

(a) Informal (illegal and semilegal)settlements, which are either already consolidated or are in various stages of consolidation. Because of the inadequate public and private supply of housing for lower social classes, these usually are and were developed by the residents themselves, so that self-help projects have tacitly become a normative component of state housing policy. The relationships between the establishment and development of these peripheral urban extensions and immigration into the city are very complex, and they are very closely connected to intraurban migration flows (BÄHR 1986, MERTINS 1985).

(b) Government-sponsored building projects. These are, for one, settlements with anywhere from a hundred to several thousand conventionally built housing units consisting of four or fivestory apartment buildings or single-family (attached) houses, usually for members of the lower-middle and middle classes. Ones for lower-class households have lower standards (size of lots and housing units, infrastructure). On the other hand, since the middle or late 1970s large sites and services and core housing settlements are increasingly being established, for financial and sociopolitical reasons. It is left up to the residents to construct huts/ houses and to add on to or consolidate them.

(c) To a lesser extent upper-class residential areas as well. Some of these have also developed informally, their location often originally determined by small weekend or summer house settlements. More recently a shopping center constructed fair in advance of the current settlement "front" is often the decisive impulse for the construction or extension of upper-class districts and thus for the areal growth of cities.

Whereas we previously had to rely on qualitative observations to explain the model, there have meanwhile been quantitatively oriented analyses, though still rather few for lack of appropriate data, which confirm the basic features of the model. It must suffice here to mention three example (for further studies with explicit reference to the model cf. BÄHR 1978, CUSTERS and VREMAN 1988, KÖSTER 1988, SCHUURMAN 1986).

1. Lima 1981 (Fig. 2; cluster analysis for 794 *zonas* on the basis of 30 variables related to socioeconomic status and position in the life cycle; after BÄHR and KLÜCKMANN 1985): it is easy to distinguish the sector with the high-class residential areas. The lay of the coast has caused this development axis to veer off at a conspicuous angle. It is also easy to recognize the cellular, frayed out structure at the outskirts ot the town, with recent squatter settlements as the chief characteristic element. The central-peripheral social gradient of the colonial city is, however, hardly aparent anymore. In contrast to other large metropolises, the residential areas near the center are for the most part rundown and consist primarily of slum-like districts, but also of older squatter settlements that are very densely populated and built-up meanwhile.

2. Recife 1970 (Fig. 3; regionalization of 454 census districts by rank correlation on the basis of 7 socioeconomic variables; after REUFELS 1988). Recife's coastal location predestines it to be subdivided into sectors with two main

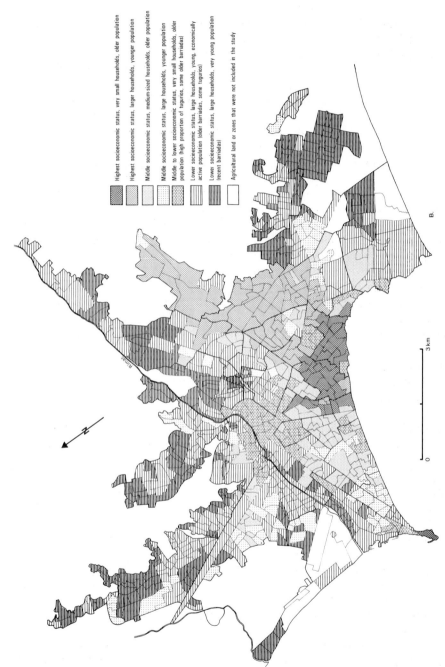

Highest socioeconomic status, very small households, older population

Highest socioeconomic status, larger households, younger population

Middle socioeconomic status, medium-sized households, older population

Middle socioeconomic status, large households, younger population

Middle to lower socioeconomic status, very small households, older population (high proportion of tugurios, some older barriadas)

Lower socioeconomic status, large households, young, economically active population (older barriadas, some tugurios)

Lower socioeconomic status, large households, very young population (recent barriadas)

Agricultural land or zones that were not included in the study

Fig. 2: Classification of the zonas of Lima/Callao according to socioeconomic status and life cycle 1980 (Source: Bähr and Klückmann 1985)

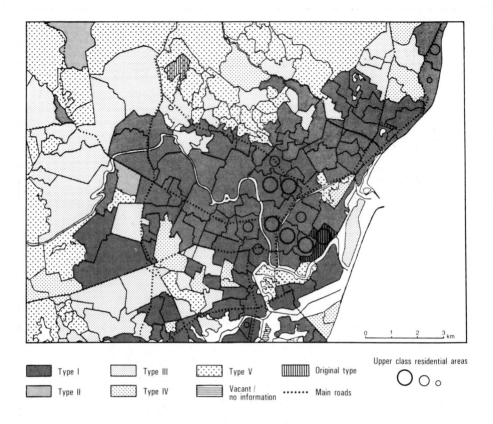

Type I	Type III	Type V	Original type
Type II	Type IV	Vacant / no information	•••••• Main roads

Upper class residential areas

Fig. 3: Classification of the census districts of Recife according to socioeconomic status 1970 (The sequence from type I to type V approximately corresponds a sequence from higher to lower socioeconomic status) (Source: Reufels 1988)

growth axes leading northward and southward. Consequently, the modern high-class residential areas lie mainly south of the map section shown here. Contrasting conspicuously with Lima, high status residential areas are still also found in downtown locations (they are represented in Figure 3 by circles), so that one can to a certain degree still speak of a socioeconomic gradient from the center toward the periphery. Residential areas for lower social classes are not found in central locations except as small isolated "islands." They are concentrated in swampy areas susceptible to flooding around river mouths.

3. Manizales 1986 (Fig. 4; social regionalization by weigthing 54 variables relating to location, dominant house type, building substance, technical and social infrastructure, traffic connections, etc., for each block/*manzana*; after Bischoff 1988).

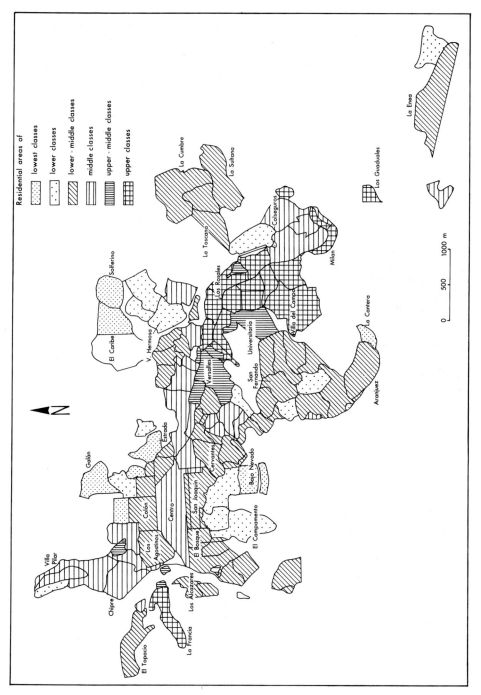

Fig. 4: Social regionalization of Manizales/Colombia 1986 (Source: Bischoff 1988)

We can clearly recognize that the social gradient from the center to the periphery is in the process of disintegration. On the one hand, the upper and upper-middle classes have already left the center, but like in the other residential areas close to the center, no slums have developed. On the other hand, the traditional residential, industrial and commercial zone around the center with lower-middle class and, to some extent, lower-class housing is still quite evident. The lower class areas lie almost exclusively in the outkirts. Their cellular appearance is partially due to Manizales' location (areas separated by deep erosion guillies, some of which have steep slopes).

Although our model has basically been confirmed as an approach to explaining spatiotemporal processes of structural and functional urban development, it still needs to be expanded, differentiated and modified today. Attention needs to be paid both to some types of urban settlement structure and to some recent types of processes that play an important role in social and functional regionalization.

We cannot, for instance, speak simply of districts with government-sponsored housing. When dealing with government housing projects of the classical, Western European type, we must distinguish according to size (number of housing units) and type of building (e.g., high-rise buildings, 4−5 story apartment buildings, single family/duplex attached house settlements), bearing in mind that these projects all have in common that they do not reach the lower 30−35 % of the urban income hierarchy. And the model must consider the new types of low-income housing settlements/districts, which have rapidly increased in number and significance since the HABITAT conference in 1976 in Vancouver: site and services, core housing settlements and settlements with small low-cost housing units (50−60 qm) and minimal infrastructure.

In differentiating these recent urban of metropolitan types of districts we drew heavily on variables relating to settlement structure. At the same time these settlement types play a very important role in the rapid areal growth of Latin American cities/metropolises. They are already an extremely characteristic element of these cities, and they affect and modify the organizational pattern at the periphery of urban settlements very highly; i.e., they are an important component of the dynamic processes occurring there.

The recent dynamic development will be outlined below using the examples of three types of processes that have caused considerable modifications in the three dominant spatial and functional patterns of Latin American cities in the past 10−15 years (Tables 1−3).

These new types of structures and processes, to which we have referred only briefly, supplement and modify our model of the Latin American city; to what extent this will happen remains for more extensive studies to show.

Table 1: Recent types of spatial and functional processes in the *inner-city mixed zone* of Latin American cities

CBD buildings and functions advance rapidly along main streets and/or around international hotel complexes. →	Former population (usually lower-class households) is displaced. High-class business and offices grow-up; apartment houses (for members of the upper-middle and upper class) are built.
Tertiary activies spread to former upper-class, now middle-class areas (sometimes only in patches). →	Single family houses/villas are transformed into office buildings (branch offices and representatives of firms), some are torn down and high-rise buildings constructed to be used for service (office) and residential purposes.
Inner-city residential areas (partially slums) and industrial zones are cleared. →	(a) Former population (usually lower-class househoulds) is displaced and area used for business. (b) In areas that have been totally cleared, modern residential districts and some specialty shops are built ("gentrification"). (c) Where buildings are rehabilitated and renovated: transformation for use for services (branch offices, representatives of firms), cultural and touristic functions.

Table 2: Recent types of spatial and functional processes in the *upper-class districts* of Latin American cities

Spatial disintegration of the upper-class "sector." →	Bungalow/chalet estates, some dispersed, some isolated, but closed off (with guards!), ahead of the upper-class "sector." Elite residential districts "remodeled" (in some cases for mixed use),
Construction of luxury apartments in high-rise buildings increase (as a precaution!). →	along/near main highway, sometimes concentrated around subway stations, in rehabilitated inner-city districts (some "working" second homes)
Tertiary activities spread along main streets. →	Single-family houses/villas transformed, some torn down and new buildings constructed with high-class services.
Shopping and recreational centers grow up, some far ahead of the upper-class "sector." →	Direction and intensity of expansion of upper-class residential districts are reinforced. Subsequently high-class subcenters grow up (with hotels, restaurants, agencies, shops, etc.).

Table 3: Recent types of spatial and functional processes in *low-income housing settlements* in Latin American cities

Changes or improvements in buildings and infrastructure made almost exclusely by the residents.	→ Buildings consolidated, residential density increases (renting out!), services improve (small shops, repair shops, etc.).
Exchange of population:	
(a) number of lower-middle class/middle class households increases (because ownership terms are too stiff for the original target group);	→ More rapid consolidation, improved services, etc.
(b) number of lower-class households increase due to renting/subrenting (in some cases after the owners have moved out).	→ Buildings and infrastructure deteriorate (particularly in core housing areas), subsequently slum development.

References:

BÄHR, J. (1976): Neuere Entwicklungstendenzen lateinamerikanischer Großstädte. Geographische Rundschau 28, 125–133.

BÄHR, J. (1978): Santiago de Chile. Eine faktoranalytische Untersuchung zur inneren Differenzierung einer lateinamerikanischen Millionenstadt. Mannheimer Geographische Arbeiten 4, Mannheim.

BÄHR, J. (1986): Innerstädtische Wanderungsbewegungen unterer Sozialschichten und peripheres Wachstum lateinamerikanischer Metropolen mit Beispielen aus Santiago de Chile und Lima). In: KOHUT, K. (ed.): Die Metropolen in Lateinamarika – Hoffnung und Bedrohung für den Menschen. Eichstätter Beiträge 18, Regensburg, 143–177.

BÄHR and J. KLÜCKMANN, G. (1985): Sozialräumliche Differenzierung von Wohngebieten unserer Einkommensgruppen in lateinamerikanischen Metropolen: Die Beispiele Santiago de Chile und Lima. Ibero-Amerikanisches Archiv, N.F. 11, 283–314.

BÄHR, J. and MERTINS, G. (1981) Idealschema der sozialräumlichen Differenzierung lateinamerikanischer Großstädte. Geographische Zeitschrift 69, 1–33.

BISCHOFF, B. (1988): Stadtentwicklung und sozialräumliche Gliederung von Manziales (Kolumbien). Staatsexamensarbeit, Marburg/L. (unpublished).

BORSDORF, A. (1976): Valdivia und Osorno. Strukturelle Disparitäten in chilenischen Mittelstädten. Tübinger Geographische Studien 69, Tübingen.

CUSTERS, G. and VREMAN, D. (1988): Housing characteristics and mobility patterns of tugurio inhabitantes in Arequipa/Southern Peru. In: BÄHR, J. (ed.): Wohnen in lateinamerikanischen Städten. Kieler Geographische Schriften 68, Kiel, 145–156.

GORMSEN, E. (1981): Die Städte im spanischen Amerika. Ein zeiträumliches Entwicklungsmodell der letzten hundert Jahre. Erdkunde 35, 290–303.

KÖSTER, G. (1988): Modelle innerstädtischer Migration gehobener Bevölkerungsgeschichten – Das Beispiel La Paz/Bolivien. In: BÄHR, J. (ed:): Wohnen in lateinamerikanischen Städten. Kieler Geographische Schriften 68, Kiel, 61–77.

MERTINS, G. (1980): Typen inner- und randstädtischer Elendsviertel in Großstädten des andinen Südamerika. In: STEGER, H.-A. & SCHNEIDER, J. (eds.): Venezuela –

Kolumbien – Ekuador. Wirtschaft, Gesellschaft und Geschichte. Lateinamerika Studien 7, München, 269–295.

MERTINS, G. (1985): Raumzeitliche Phasen intraurbaner Migration unterer Sozialschichten in lateinamerikanischen Großstädten. Ibero-Amerikanisches Archiv, N.F. 11, 315–332.

MERTINS, G. (1991): Contribuciones al modelo de diferenciación socioespacial de ciudades intermedias de América Latina: ejemplos colombianos. Revista Interamericana de Planificación 24 (93), 172–194.

REUFELS, U. (1988): Zur sozialräumlichen Gliederung von Groß-Recife/Nordostbrasilien 1970–1980. In: BÄHR, J. (ed.): Wohnen in lateinamerikanischen Städten. Kieler Geographische Schriften 68, Kiel, 1–15.

SCHUURMAN, F. J. (1986): John Turner revisited. An intra-urban migration model for colonial-type cities in Latin America. Tijdschrift voor Economische en Sociale Geografie 77, 221–230.

WILHELMY, H. and BORSDORF, A. (1984): Die Städte Südamerikas. Teil 1. Wesen und Wandel. Urbanisierung der Erde 3/1, Berlin/Stuttgart.

THE CITIES OF TROPICAL AFRICA – CROSS-CULTURAL ASPECTS, DESCRIPTIVE MODELS AND RECENT DEVELOPMENTS

With 7 figures

Walther Manshard

1. Introduction

Although Africa is one of the less urbanized continents, the annual growth rate of its urban population of about 5 % (representing a doubling time of only 12 years) lies well over the average general growth rate of its population (of about 3 %) and reaches a high level even compared to other developing regions of the world. It has been estimated that the urban population of Africa will rise from about 220 million at the beginning of the 1990's to over 340 million at the end of the twentieth century.

At present Africa's urban population accounts for about one third of the total population (in 1950 only 11 %), and it is expected that this figure will rise above 50 % at the beginning of the next century. If this trend continues Africa's urban population in 2025 may be three times that of North America. Besides high birth rates, this is largely due to rural-urban migration, because urban centres generally offer more working possibilities, better health and education facilities and a safer food supply in times of crises. An important characteristic part of the general urbanization process is obviously the increased concentration of the population in a number of metropolitan centres and primate cities. (Fig. 1). An example: In Ghana about one third of the urban population is concentrated in the Accra-Tema region (1984: 1,2 mill.). In Dakar (Senegal), Cotonou (Benin) or Lomé (Togo) about two thirds of the urban populations live in the capital.

| | 1950 | | 1960 | | 1970 | | 1975 | | 1980 | |
	(1)	(2)	(1)	(2)	(1)	(2)	(1)	(2)	(1)	(2)
Senegal	21,7	46,s	22,6	52,8	23,7	60,1	24,2	64,0	25,4	64,9
Ivory Coast	13,0	–	19,3	27,2	27,7	29,9	32,6	31,6	37,6	32,6
Ghana	14,5	38,1	23,2	25,1	29,1	30,0	32,3	32,9	35,9	34,5
Togo	7,2	–	9,8	–	13,1	58,4	15,1	60,0	17,4	60,4
Benin	6,6	–	9,5	–	16,0	47,4	23,0	56,6	30,8	62,9
Nigeria	10,5	–	13,1	2,1	16,4	4,4	18,2	6,4	20,4	7,9
Cameroon	9,8	34,3	13,9	25,6	20,3	21,1	27,2	20,9	34,6	21,5
Mali	8,1	–	11,1	31,9	14,9	32,2	17,2	33,9	19,9	34,3
Sudan	6,3	31,1	10,3	30,3	16,4	30,0	20,4	30,1	24,8	30,6
Zaire	19,1	8,8	22,3	14,2	30,3	20,9	34,9	25,4	40,0	28,0
Angola	7,6	44,5	10,4	39,9	15,0	54,8	17,8	61,5	21,0	63,6
Kenya	5,6	41,4	7,4	28,9	10,2	48,0	12,0	54,1	14,2	57,3

Fig. 1: Urban population in percent of total population (1) and proportion of primate cities of urban population (2) in selected African countries (after UN 1980)

2. Cross-cultural Typology

At first sight the complex cultural identity of urban centres in Tropical Africa can be defined by using a number of dichotonomies, with terms such as traditional/modern, indigenous/alien, autochthonous/allochthonous, orthogenetic/heterogenetic (REDFIELD and SINGER 1954). In Africa this more descriptive analysis is easier to grasp than in other parts of the world, since over one century of colonial domination has had a strong influence on both physical infrastructure and social life style. Some exceptions exist from this rather one-sided colonial "imprint" such as the African rural towns in the Yoruba lands of Western Nigeria, the emirates of Northern Nigeria or other precolonial cities in the Sudano-Sahelian zone, where urban centres developed both from African and Oriental roots, but were strongly modified later. There were also developments in connection with Arab-Indian influences in Kenya or Tanzania, the original quasi-urban structures in Ethiopia (KULS 1970), or the special case of old "Zimbabwe".

The pre-colonial era with its social and political organization was mainly characterised by a formation of ethnically segregated urban quarters, in which kinship ties and also subsystems of professional differentiation dominated.

For Tropical Africa a number of important urban types can be distinguished, and most cities are structurally and functionally made up by a "mix" of these elements (O'CONNOR 1983, MANSHARD 1977).

1. The traditional African town (e.g. in West Africa) often was an indigenous centre of administration for local chiefs and "kings".

2. Islamic centres developed with strong cultural connections to North Africa, or in the case of East Africa, to Arabia and Persia.

This historic-cultural classification has to be complemented by considering the changes in regional importance, e.g. the reversal of the originally peripheral maritime locations at the Guinea Coast, which changed in economic and political importance, with European colonisation since the 16th century, vis-á-vis the continental centres of the Western Sudan based on Trans-Saharan trade.

This historical background is vital to an understanding of the cultural development of West African cities. In almost all colonial territories, which were carved – usually quite arbitrarily – out of the amorphous African block, from Senegal to the Cameroons, this contrast between two distinct ways of life can be observed. On the one hand, the attitude to life found at the coast, which was receptive to ideas from Europe, and which had a strong antipathy towards everthing coming from the "bush" of the African hinterland. On the other hand, the attitude to life found in the Sudanic zone, which, hearing in mind the strong stamp of Islam, was much more closely attached to tradition. Even today some of the political problems facing these states can be connected to these long-standing differences.

3. The Colonial city with its dualistic structure between "ville noire" and "ville blanche" increasingly changed into (4.) more hybrid cities. More "European-

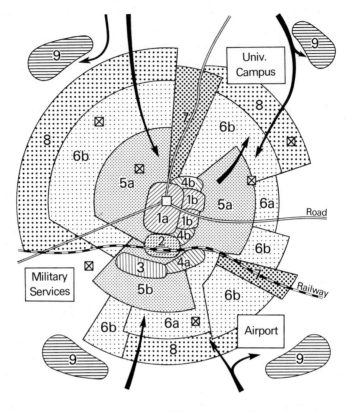

Fig. 2: Basic pattern of urban development in tropical Africa (MANSHARD 1991)

1a Dominant ethnic nucleus (often within walls with traditional political and religious institutions)
1b Other ethnic African quarters
2 Central Business District (CBD)
3 Central Administration District (CAD)
4a Former European quarter
4b Other foreign quarters (e.g. Lebanese / Syrians in West Africa)
5a Mixed residential area, mostly lower or middle level
5b Mixed residential area, middle to upper level
6a Planned suburban development, mostly middle level
6b Lower level residential
7 Industrial area
8 Suburban zone (mostly lower level)
9 Spontaneous squatter settlements (outside of city)
□ Main traditional market
⊠ Subcentres / smaller markets
➤ Directions of migration

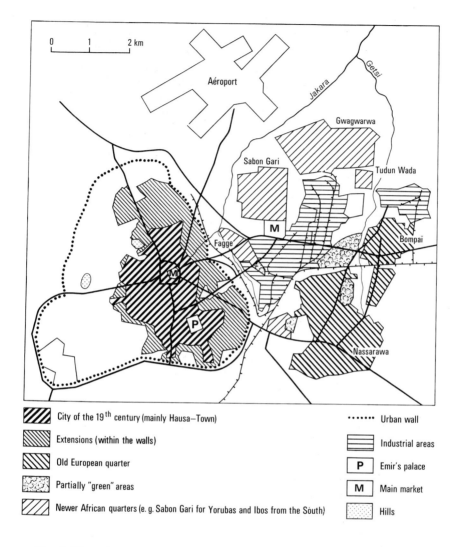

▨ City of the 19th century (mainly Hausa–Town)	⋯⋯ Urban wall
▧ Extensions (within the walls)	☰ Industrial areas
◤ Old European quarter	P Emir's palace
░ Partially "green" areas	M Main market
▨ Newer African quarters (e. g. Sabon Gari for Yorubas and Ibos from the South)	⣿ Hills

Fig. 3: Kano (at the end of the 1960s) (after BECKER 1969 and VENNETIER 1976)

type" towns (5.) or centres with a more Indian background developed in Southern and Eastern Africa (e.g. Harare; formerly Salisbury, Bulawayo in Zimbabwe, or Nairobi in Kenya.).

Fig. 2 presents a simple model describing the genetic structure of an average African city of an "hybrid" type, based more on urban growth of (ex-British) West Africa, and blending it with a synthesis of the functional development in the colonial and post colonial period.

79

Similar structural patterns are demonstrated by Fig. 3 (Kano) and Fig. 4 (Ibadan), while Fig. 5 (Dar-es-Salaam) shows the East African variety with stronger Indian components.

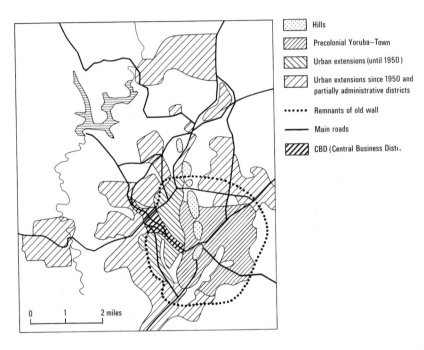

Fig. 4: Basic urban pattern of Ibadan (Nigeria) (after Udo 1970 and Vennetier 1976)

In West Africa the old "native" town was often dominated by a single ethnic group, while further quarters belonged to other groups. These quarters often had their own social hierarchiy, local administration, and market rights. They continued and survived even into colonial times, e.g. the Sabon Garis in Nigeria or the Zongos in Ghana. During this period the influence of European expatriates and "colonial intermediatries" ("koloniale Zwischenschichten") such as Indians in East Africa, Lebanese/Syrians in West Africa and Greeks in Central Africa increased both in numbers and in economic importance. However, during the final phase of colonial rule, ethnic (and even racial) differences increasingly disappeared. They were replaced by new forms of social segregation based on income and education.

Very typical for the whole of Africa was the extraordinary mobility of the population. This mobility, expressed in migratory movements of widely varying volume in both ancient and modern times, was difficult to assess statistically. Very

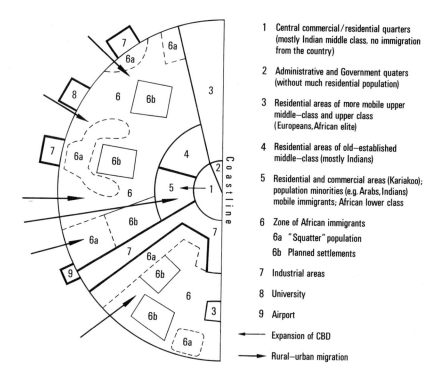

1 Central commercial/residential quarters (mostly Indian middle class, no immigration from the country)

2 Administrative and Government quaters (without much residential population)

3 Residential areas of more mobile upper middle—class and upper class (Europeans, African elite)

4 Residential areas of old—established middle—class (mostly Indians)

5 Residential and commercial areas (Kariakoo); population minorities (e.g. Arabs, Indians) mobile immigrants; African lower class

6 Zone of African immigrants
    6a "Squatter" population
    6b Planned settlements

7 Industrial areas

8 University

9 Airport

← Expansion of CBD

→ Rural—urban migration

Fig. 5: Schematic pattern of social areas in Dar-es-Salaam (modified after VORLAUFER 1973)

important was, for example, the migration of the Mossi and other groups from the middle Niger in Mali to the coast, to Ghana and the Ivory Cost. Another such migration route transcending all colonial frontiers ran from Northern Nigeria into the Sudan (Khartoum), and then on to Mecca. Corresponding to their origin, the majority of itinerant workers was engaged in agriculture. They worked as labourers and contract workers on plantations or on farms. A large number, however, reached the cities, where due to their minimal wages, they constituted the lowest class of unskilled labourers. The process of urbanization in Africa and Europe shows similarities and differences. Although the African cities have had a magnetic attraction for their closer and more distant hinterland, and although one can discern rural depopulation and the growth of "slums" as phenomena with a high degree of similarity to our European cities of the 18th and 19th century, in Africa it was generally not industry but trade, which stood in the centre of development. Thus the magic formulas for urbanization were trade and in some cases political administration and not industrialization.

81

The majority of the cities grew up as ports or as transport nodes within important production areas for export commodities. Often they were located at points where lines of communication were interrupted. Their major functions consisted in the export of tropical products and the various ores, which the traders exchanged for European consumer goods. The urban foci and "symbols" were, therefore, often of a commercial nature. What the cathedrals and guildhalls were in the townscapes of medieval Europe, and the mosques and bazaars of the Arab world, these were represented in Tropical Africa by the European stores and commercial establishments, which developed from the old factories. Following the economic development in colonial times new structures were superimposed on the old patterns, where also tradtional markets played an important role. Modern "Central Business Districts and Central Administrative Districts" (CBDs/CADs) attracted new functions, different types of residential areas emerged and new forms of transportation and industries developed. These new patterns can to some extent be linked to urban models developed in North America (e.g. BURGESS 1925; HOYT 1939; HARRIS/ULLMAN 1945).

So far there exists no comprehensive model of the African city in general. Only for individual cities, often in connection with monographs, attempts were made in this direction (e.g. VORLAUFER, 1973: Dar-es-salaam; BECKER, 1969: Kano; UDO, 1970: Ibadan; HINDERINK and STERKENBURG, 1975: Cape Coast). In contrast to the fairly well investigated pre-colonial and colonial patterns, the information about recent developments is rather scanty. It is hoped that research undertaken by a German team (GAEBE, HENKEL, VORLAUFER, to be published in the „Zeitschrift für Wirtschaftsgeographie" in 1991) will lead to some results in this direction. Fig. 2 aims at a preliminary abstraction that encompasses ideas of the North American zonal-, sectoral-, and multi-nuclei approaches mentioned above, as well as some new developments summarized by MABOGUNJE (1986) stressing processes such as backwash urbanization and peasantization.

3. Postcolonial Developments: Backwash Urbanization and Peasantization

With the dissolution of colonial structures the economic and social polarization between urban centres and rural areas became more evident. Members of the new African élites often took over the former residential accommodation of colonial administrators, though in some countries (e.g. Ivory Coast or Gabon) the influence of foreign advisers and business people even increased after political independence in the early 1960's. Political developments varied from socialist-marxist countries (e.g. Guinea, Benin, Mocambique, Congo-Brazzaville) to states oriented more towards Western market economies (e.g. Ivory Coast, Kenya, Gabon). With the resulting economic situation, labour migration towards urban centres increased not only within but also between countries and regions. In fact, these large scale labour movements had already begun in colonial times. The attractiveness of metropolitan centres and primate cities caused millions of African peasants to move. Ecological catastrophies (Sahel) often coupled with famines and civil wars (Angola, Ethiopia, Mocambique, Sudan, Liberia, Tchad, Somalia) accentuated this trend. It is interesting to note that in recent times the "push factors" behind rural-urban migration are becoming more important than the traditional "pull factors".

The "backwash-effect" of both inappropriate policies and economic programs expressed itself also in increased urbanization. "The most visible manifestation of this "backwash-urbanization" is the environment situation in many African cities... The gulf between what governments would like to do with such areas and what they actually are able to do underscores the extent to which African cities have been "peasantized". This reflects both the "peasants" of rural origin of immigrants as well as the "peasant-type" strategies to survive, albeit new within an urban environment." (MABOGUNJE 1986, pp. 268–69).

In general terms "backwash urbanization" has been defined as a kind of resurgence of migrants from a city into the surrounding countryside, because of the decrease of attractiveness of the original destination of this migration. In this process a diffuse "rurban" zone may develop in the periphery of the city, sometimes leading to the formation of new small centers. The difference between backwash urbanization and suburbanization is, that the latter rather represents an inward-out movement, while the processes of the former are more a "reflection" of the centrifugal "waves" of immigrants. Also several forms of peasantization can be distinguished. Sometimes the term may also be used for the processes of "submergence" of existing rural communities by rapid urbanization.

As a result the new rural-urban interfaces are mostly very complex, and the roots of urban populations in Tropical-Africa through cultural, ethnic and even religious links to the country are still stronger than in most other regions of the developing world.

Peri-urban and semi-rural zones of transition with squatter settlements (bidonvilles, shanty towns) have emerged. Again these had already begun to grow during the colonial period. They were used by migrants as a kind of catalytic "transit station" between the country and the "melting pot" of the city. In the 1960s and 70s the urban "informal sector" increased considerably. It is difficult to give exact figures about the number of people living under marginal sub-standard housing conditions. In most African cities this proportion can be estimated to be between 30–70 % (For the 1980s estimates were: Addis Abada 80 %: Ibadan 60 %, cf. also Fig. 6 after MERTINS 1984). Although urban migrants try to upgrade their housing conditions, with or without governmental help, the rapid pace of inward migration constantly exceeds the available sources of finance. Investments in urban infrastructure such as transportation and sanitation systems never have had time to catch up. (CAMP 1991).

Metropole (Country)	Proportion (in %)
Accra (Ghana)	53
Dakar (Senegal)	60
Daressalam (Tanzania)	35
Kinshasa (Zaire)	60
Lagos (Nigeria)	51
Lusaka (Zambia)	58
Nairobi (Kenya)	48

Fig. 6: Proportion (in percent of urban population living in "slums" or "shanty towns" in African metropolitan cities (after MERTINS 1984)

On the other hand, prestige buildings (e.g. the presidential palaces in Abidjan, Libreville or Conakry or the new cathedrals in Abidjan and Yamassoukrou) were erected in many countries. Modern CBDs with shopping centres and supermarkets developed side by side with tradition markets. CAD's developed out of administrative structures often dating back to colonial times. During recent years the situation in African cities has reached critical dimensions. The urban organization has shown an increasing "erosion of social discipline" (MABOGUNJE 1990). Urban services (e.g. electricity, water supply, refuse collection) have tended to break down especially in the poorer and peripheral zones. Crime rates and urban violence have increased. Security for persons and property could no longer be guaranteed. Urban and state governments have tried, so far with little success, to mobilize their citizens against this social disintegration. In some cases (Nigeria) neighbourhood organizations were proposed, in which links were attempted back to traditional forms (stressing kinship-ties) of pre-colonial times.

Economic problems, like the increased debt burden or the oil crisis, contributed to the breakdown of the agricultural market-system. This did not allow the cities to recuperate and to play their proper role as "growth-poles" and hubs of distribution. Even oil-rich countries like Nigeria, which tried to compensate their excessive dependency on imports by a strict "selective closure"-policy, failed in their attempts to improve their situation. In most cases counter-measures by IMF and World Bank and drastic devaluations of national currencies did not really succed "to turn the wheel around". It is an interesting problem how African city dwellers react to the structural IMF-measures. Some, may, even more than before, be obliged to join the informal sector, some manage to get jobs in the new industrial enterprises of the formal sector, others even have to leave the city and either emigrate to another country or some go back to traditional agriculture in their villages of origin.

All this is reflected by a growing assymmetry between urban centres and rural areas. In spite of some dynamic impetus from urban growth-poles the transfer of resources from the country to the city, mostly through increased migration, had rather negative results. Therefore the "urban bias of development" (LIPTON 1977, 1984) in Africa was not really a success story. "Polarization reversal" (RICHARDSON 1980) with increased importance of the small and medium centres did not take place either or remained rather weak (e.g. the failure of the "Ujamaa System" in Tanzania). The unwillingness of urban élites to agree to drastic policy changes in the rural sector contributed to the present difficulties. Urban trade unions managed to obtain higher wages, which in turn increased the deficits of trade balances between the city and its agricultural hinterland. Changed consumption patterns (increased import of wheat-flour for bread, of rice and milk instead of local foodstuffs) further widened the gap between urban and rural areas.

No "return to the land", as one element of a beginning "counter-urbanization", can so far be observed in Africa. Only in some cases members of the upper social groups (e.g. politicians, business-men) have started to operate in the country, where – mostly as absentee land-lords – they often bought land in order to start modern agricultural enterprises (e.g. market gardening, poultry and pig-farming etc.).

In connection with large scale shifts of people from rural to urban settings, the processes of urbanization can also be linked to "peasantization" with its various forms of urban- and periurban agriculture. Lower income groups, especially female migrants, improved their cash income by establishing home- or market gardens. Even urban livestock keeping (cattle, sheep) is fairly common. Some governments encourage (e.g. in the "Feed Yourself-Campaigns" in Ghana) members of the middle classes to establish urban subsistence gardens. Although cities obviously are mainly centres of food consumption, experience has shown that in times of economic crises urban agriculture can be quite successful.

An important and interesting feature of modern African cities is the restructuring of the urban periphery. "La ville est en train d'urbaniser son proche arrière pays" (VENNETIER 1986). House building – together with the transportation sector – still considered to be the most stable form of capital investment, leads to new diffuse structures in the suburban periphery. At another social level spontenous squatting settlements ("quartiers spontannés") have developed side by side with well-planned modern quarters (e.g. the "lotissements" in francophone Africa).

4. Summary and Conclusion

Structurally and functionally different socio-economic preferences have found a spatial expression in African cities. While in precolonial time ethnic quarters dominated, in the colonial and postcolonial period often geometric patterns of planning and building prevailed. Most cities in Africa reflect in their identity these cross cultural historic relationships.

The key questions of coping with changing social structure, with land reforms and deteriorating environmental conditions have to be solved at a political level. However, for this reason a better understanding of the main problems is needed. More surveys and inventories using more specific morphological, taxonomic, genetic and spatial criteria are essential for a newly defined typology of African cities, stressing the important regional differences within the continent (Fig. 7).

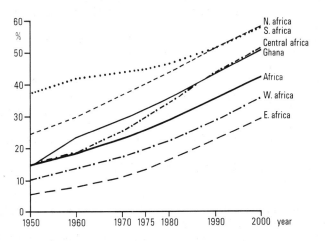

Fig. 7: Development of urban population as part of the total population in Africa (1950–2000) (after UN 1980 and Thomi 1989)

This should include assessments and indicators of different levels of urban development with more detailed studies of public health and safety, housing standards and living space, communication, education and environment (e.g. water- and air pollution, traffic congestion, noise). It is typical that in an assessment of the hundred largest cities of the world the only two African "Mega"-Cities (Lagos and Kinshasa) had the absolute lowest score (Camp 1991).

From 1900 to 1990 the world population has about tripled. During the same time the economic output has approximately increased by the factor 20. With this global perspective in mind, a much better knowledge of the world's processes of urbanization is needed encompassing the whole hierarchy from primate-cities to small sub-urban settlements. Also the aspect of the "Human Dimension of Global Change" is important for our better understanding of the earth's "Nature of Cities"; so ably portrayed by Chauncy D. Harris.

86

Bibliography:

BÄHR, J.: Neue Entwicklungstendenzen lateinamerikanischer Großstädte. In: Geographische Rundschau (28), 1976, pp. 125−33.

BÄHR, J. and MERTINS, G.: Idealschema der sozialräumlichen Differenzierung lateinamerikanischer Großstädte. In: Geographische Zeitschrift 69, 1981, pp. 1−33.

BECKER, C.: Kano − eine afrikanische Großstadt. Hamburg 1969.

BENNEH, G.: Urbanization in Africa. In: IUCN Bull. Vol. 21 (2), Gland 1990, pp. 15−16.

BORSDORF, A.: Die lateinamerikanische Großstadt. In: Geographische Rundschau 34, 1982, pp. 498−501.

BURGESS, E. W.: The Growth of the City − An Introduction to a Research Project. In: PARK, R. E. and BURGESS, E. W. (eds.): The City. Chicago 1925.

CAMPS. S. L. (ed.) Cities. Life in the World's 100 Largest Metropolitan Areas. Population Crisis Committee. Washington 1991.

GAEBE, W., HENKEL, R. and VORLAUFER, K.: Urbanisierungsprozesse in schwarzafrikanischen Städten. Manuskript Antrag VW-Stiftung 1986.

GAEBE, W.: Verdichtungsräume. Stuttgart 1987.

GORMSEN, E.: Die Städte im spanischen Amerika. Ein zeit-räumliches Entwicklungsmodell der letzten 100 Jahre. In: Erdkunde 35, 1981, pp. 290−303.

GUYER, J. J. (ed.): Feeding African Cities: Studies in Regional and Social History. Manchester 1987.

HARRIS, C. D.: A Functional Classification of Cities in the United States. In: Geographical Review 33, 1943, pp. 86−99.

HARRIS, C. D. and ULLMAN, E. L.: The Nature of Cities. In: Ann. Am. Acad. Pol. Sciences, 1945, pp. 7−17.

HEINRITZ, G.: Zentralität und zentrale Orte. Stuttgart 1979.

HENKEL, R.: Nationale Städtesysteme im östlichen und südlichen Afrika. In: Zeitschrift für Wirtschaftsgeographie 39, 1986, pp. 14−26.

HINDERINK, J. and STERKENBURG, J.: Anatomy of an African Town. Utrecht 1965.

HOFMEISTER, B.: Die Stadtstruktur. Ihre Ausprägung in den verschiedenen Kulturräumen der Erde. Darmstadt 1980.

ibid.: Stadtgeographie. Braunschweig, 1980.

HOYT, H.: The Structure and Growth of Residential Neighbourhoods in American Cities. Washington 1939.

International Monetary Fund (I.M.F.): World Economic Outlook. Washington 1982, p. 97.

KULS, W.: Zur Entwicklung städtischer Siedlungen in Äthiopien. In: Erdkunde 24, 1970, pp. 14−26.

LICHTENBERGER, E.: Perspektiven der Stadtgeographie. In: Abhandlungen des 42. deutschen Geographentages Göttingen 1979, pp. 103−28.

ibid.: Stadtgeographie − Perspektiven. In: Geographische Rundschau 38, 1986, pp. 388−94.

ibid.: Stadtgeographie − Begriffe, Konzepte, Modelle, Prozesse. Stuttgart 1986.

LIPTON, M.: Why People Stay Poor − Urban Bias to World Development. London 1977.

ibid.: Urban Bias Revisited. In: Journal of Development Studies 29, 1984, pp. 139−:66.

MABOGUNJE, A. L.: Urbanization in Nigeria. London 1969.

ibid.: Africa − After a False Start. Vortrag I.G.U. Conference, Sydney 1988.

87

ibid.: The Organization of Urban Communities in Nigeria. In: Tales of Cities, ISSC. Paris 1990, pp. 355–366.

MANSHARD, W.: A Simple Teaching Model Explaining the Spatial Differentiation of Urban Functions. In: Bull. Ghana Geogr. Ass. 1960, pp. 21–24 und Geoforum 1970, pp. 93–94.

ibid.: Die Stadt Kumasi – Stadt und Umland in ihrer funktionalen Beziehung. In: Erdkunde 15, 1961, pp. 161–80.

ibid.: Die Bedeutung der ethnisch bestimmten Viertelsbildung in den Städten Schwarzafrikas. In: Gentz-Festschrift. Kiel 1970, pp. 123–138.

ibid.: Die Städte des Tropischen Afrika. Stuttgart 1977.

ibid.: Die neuen Hauptstädte Tropisch-Afrikas. In: Zeitschrift für Wirtschaftsgeographie 30, Heft 3/4, 1986a, pp. 1–13.

ibid.: Stadt-Umwelt – und Stadt-Umlandprobleme in Tropisch-Afrika. In: Tübinger Gespräche zu Entwicklungsfragen. Tübingen 1988b, pp. 37–47.

ibid.: Hausgartenanbau in Westaufrika. In: Klaer-Festschrift. Mainz 1990, pp. 321–332.

MERTINS, G.: Marginalsiedlungen in Großstädten der Dritten Welt. In: Geogr. Rundschau 9/1984, pp. 434–443.

OBUDHO, R. A. and MHLANGA, C. C:: (eds.): Slum and Squatter Settlements in Sub-Saharan Africa: Toward a Planning Strategy. New York 1988.

O'CONNOR, A.: Urbanization in Tropical Africa – An Annotated Bibliography. Boston. 1981.

ibid.; The African City. London 1983.

PRESTELE, H. H.: Das Potential der Städte nutzen – Urbanisierung und Sekundärzentren in Schwarzafrika. In: Zeitschrift für Wirtschaftsgeographie 33, 1989, pp. 232–37.

REDFIELD, R. and SINGER, M. B.: The Cultural Role of Cities. In: Economical Development and Cultural Change 1954, pp. 53–73.

RICHARDSON, H. W.: Polarization Reversal in Developing Countries. In: Papers RSA Vol. 54, 1980, pp. 67–85.

SANTOS, M.: Spatial Dialectics – The Two Circuits of Urban Economy in Underdeveloped Countries. In: Antipode 3 1977, pp. 49–60.

SCHEFFLER R.: Wesen und Besonderheiten des Metropolisierungsprozesses in Entwicklungsländern Afrikas. In: Geographische Berichte 124, 1987, pp. 145–57.

SCHNEIDER, K. G. and WIESE, B.: Die Städte des südlichen Afrika. Stuttgart 1983.

STREN, R. E. and WHITE, R. R. (eds.): African Cities in Crisis. Boulder 1989.

THOMI, W. H.: Struktur und Funktion des produzierenden Kleingewerbes in Klein- und Mittelstädten Ghanas. Stuttgart 1989.

UDO, R. K.: The Geographical Regions of Nigeria. London 1970.

VENNETIER, P.: Les Villes d'Afrique Noire. Paris 1977.

ibid.: Evolution des espaces peri-urbains en Afrique Tropicale. CNRS-CEGET; Paper Bordeaux-Bochum 1986.

VORLAUFER, K.: Dar-es-Salaam. Hamburg 1973.

ibid.: Die Funktion der Mittelstädte Afrikas im Prozeß des sozialen Wandels. Das Beispiel Tanzania. In: Afrika Spektrum 2, 1971, pp. 41–59.

WILHELMY, H. and BORSDORF, A.: Die Städte Südamerikas. Teil 1/2. Stuttgart 1984, 1985.

WINTERS, C.: Urban Morphogenesis in Francophone Black Afrika. In: Geogr. Review 72, 1982, pp. 139–154.

THE CITY OF THE ISLAMIC MIDDLE EAST

With 7 figures and 1 table

ECKART EHLERS

1. Introductory Remarks

There seems to be little doubt and even less controversial discussion among the international community of geographers as to the characteristics and unique features of the Islamic City. According to a seemingly unanimous perception of this phenomenon, the city of the Islamic Middle East is characterized by – among others – the following features:

- a hierarchy of functions with Friday Mosque and bazaar as the spatial core of any city;
- a hierarchy of trades within the bazaar with "high ranking" trades close to the core and less esteemed trades and professions in greater distance from it;
- intra-urban residential quarters with segregation according to social, ethnic, religious and/or tribal differentiations of its inhabitants;
- military installations, fortifications, and city-gates; and finally
- very specific features such as cemeteries or periodic rural markets extra muros.

Models of the "Islamic City" in different languages and publications (cf. DETTMANN 1969; KARK 1981; SOFFER-STERN 1986, WAGSTAFF 1980 or WIRTH 1990) are more or less identical in their basic content, independent of when and where they have been published. DETTMANN's model, by far the best known and most often referred to in German geography, may serve as an example of this type of modelling of the city of the Islamic Middle East (fig. 1).

It is apparent and noteworthy, however, that there is very obviously a far reaching agreement in regard not only to what should be included in a geographical model of the city of the Islamic Middle East, but also in regard to what should not be included or what need not be discussed. Notwithstanding a few exceptions (cf. SEGER 1978, 1979), there seems to be general agreement that modelling the city of the Islamic Middle East means modelling the madina or traditional city centre. There is an equally general agreement (again with very few exceptions!) that modelling does *not* include, for example, architecture or building material as a response to unique natural and ecological conditions or other features. Equally scarce, if not entirely lacking, are attemps to include specific and eventually unique economic functions of the city (e.g. rent-capitalism) or its spatially effective religious foundations and functions.

It is therefore not surprising that basic criticism in regard to such purely descriptive, formal and superficial approaches has been formulated from outside geography. By scrutinizing the "isnad" of Western perceptions of the Middle

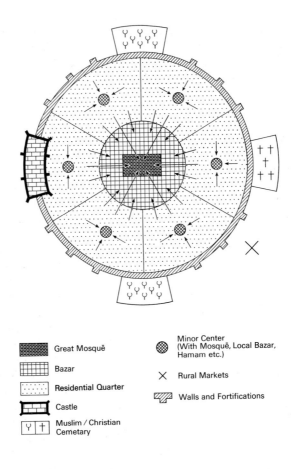

Great Mosquē		Minor Center (With Mosquē, Local Bazar, Hamam etc.)	
Bazar		Rural Markets	
Residential Quarter		Walls and Fortifications	
Castle			
Muslim / Christian Cemetary			

Fig. 1: Model of the Islamic City (after DETTMANN)

Eastern city, J. ABU-LUGHOD (1987) has demonstrated convincingly the strong impact of French orientalism on its development and its final formulation. At the same time, ABU-LUGHOD argues with good reason that decisive aspects of our perception and understanding of Middle Eastern urbanism are consequently influenced by the experience of Maghrebian urbanity by MARCAIS or BRUNSCHVIG.

This is not the place to go into details of the argumentation by J. ABU-LUGHOD or to discuss her conclusions according to which "the construction of the concept of the Islamic city was an integral part of the colonial project of distancing, objectifying, and dehumanizing the peoples who were to be treated as ‚lesser‘" (ABU-LUGHOD 1989, p. 212)

Instead, the following considerations aim at the development of a new model of the city of the Islamic Middle East. Going beyond formal description and

90

trying to incorporate both economic and religious-historical aspects, it nevertheless will miss the regional, historical, and cultural diversity of the present-day reality of urbanism of the Islamic world. It should, therefore, be stressed that the following attempt also is far from complete in covering the very essence of "what is Islamic about a city" (ABU-LUGHOD 1989).

2. The City of the Islamic Middle East: The Formal Aspect

Basic assumptions of the following considerations are
- first: there has been a kind of prototype of the "Islamic city" which may be understood as the well-known aforementioned model;
- second: this prototype is no longer existent; it is either considerable modified in its interior structure or – as a rule – it is integrated into and/or is enclosed by the modern urban fabric, which has encroached upon the traditional madinas.

It is a most interesting observation that the vast majority of all published models of the city of the Islamic Middle East (cf. fig. 1) are concentrated exclusively on the traditional city. There is hardly any attempt to comprehend the city of the Islamic Middle East as a composite of the madina *plus* its modern extensions. This is the more surprising since in many cases the old city (madina) covers only very small fractions of the whole urban fabric. As a general rule one may say: the bigger the city today, the smaller is the share of its traditional urban centre! The madina of Casablanca, for example, is but a small portion of the whole metropolis. The same holds true for Algiers, Tunis, Cairo, Istanbul, Damascus, Bagdad, Tehran, Lahore or Shahjahanabad/Delhi and many other centres of the Middle East. It would be wrong, however, to suggest that all these and other examples can or should be covered by one comprehensive model. Reality is that even the traditional cities of the Islamic Middle East reflected a wide variety of urban forms and functions. Cities vary considerably not only in regard to their historical development and regional as well cultural diversity, but also in their policies towards preservation or destruction of the madinas and with corresponding policies towards modern expansion and modernization.

Fig. 2 is an attempt to cover the diversity of regionally different urban developments in the Middle East since the late 19th century. In Turkey and Iran, the only countries with no immediate colonial past, urban reforms initiated by Atatürk and Reza Shah resulted in the transformation of the old city centres by large thoroughfares, by the demolition of the walls and by the development of new modern quarters in direct connection with the old urban fabric. Under colonial influence diverse policies were applied. The French in North Africa followed two different policies. In Marocco, for example, there was a strict separation between the madina and the "ville nouvelle" (cf. EHLERS 1984/1986). In Algeria or Tunisia, however, the French urban planners did not object to the direct juxtaposition of old and new. The British urban policy practised

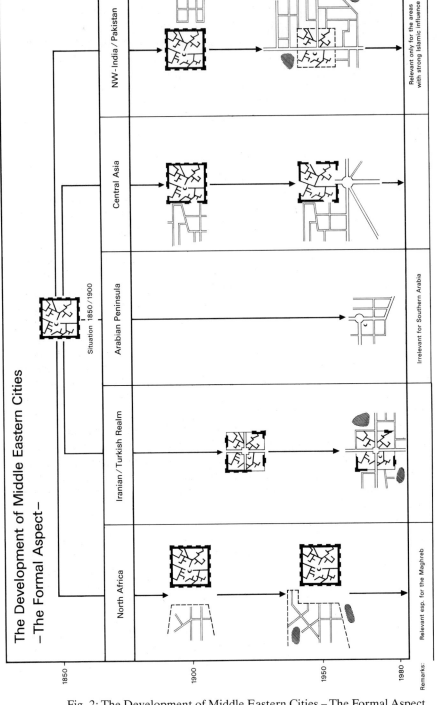

Fig. 2: The Development of Middle Eastern Cities – The Formal Aspect

segregation: cantonment and civil lines (SMAILES 1969, DETTMANN 1980) lay far away from indigenous urban centers. In Central Asia, Tsarist and Soviet rule transformed traditional cities most dramatically: besides adding colonial and socialistic forms of urban design directly to the old cores of the Islamized cities, the Soviets more or less demolished all their traditional social, economic, and religious functions (cf. GIESE 1979, 1980). In the oil-rich Arab sheikhdoms and states of the Persian Gulf, finally, the few existing traditional urban features have been more or less totally replaced by western layouts and designs so that hardly any remnants of the past are left (BONINE-CORDES 1983; CORDES-BONINE 1983; WIRTH 1988).

Already this very simple and formalistic survey reveals the problem: if there have been so many and partly dramatic formal changes in the past, what then is the city of the Islamic Middle East today? Neglecting and ignoring the aforementioned regional diversities, we can – at least – state that formally any city of the Islamic Middle East is a composite of two, or more, urban components: the traditional and the modern city. However, as the traditional urban core is separated into different quarters, so also is the modern section of the city. Residential quarters of different prestige and status are interspersed with smaller or larger shopping districts, many of which, at least in the metropoles of the Islamic Middle East, have developed into a CBD in a western sense with banks, international hotels, airline offices, department stores, restaurants, and other features so familiar from the "downtowns" of European or American cities. More or less extended industrial areas are also as typical of these modern additions to the old cores as are all those social and educational institutions, such as universities, hospitals or traffic installations (bus stations, railway yards, etc.).

In short: neither the model of the traditional city of the Islamic Middle East nor the idea of a simply dualistic structure comes close to reality. Instead, the present urban structure of the city in the Islamic Middle East is that of a multi-faceted and complex symbiosis of different forms and functions. As much as madina may be juxtaposed to ville nouvelle, as much stand bazaar and CBD, bazaar and modern industry, residential area and slums, villa and low cost housing as segments of a symbiosis, which is the modern city of the Islamic Middle East (cf. fig. 3).

The multi-functional and multi-nuclei differentation of the present-day city of the Middle East requires almost necessarily a new look also at the problem of intra-urban differentiations. Central-peripheral hierarchy is an immanent part of all traditional models and has been specifically dealt with for the bazaar in general (WIRTH 1974/1975). Reality, however, is that on the gradients of economic land-values and public evaluation within the old cities is nowadays superimposed a new economic order. The CBD of the new city ("ville nouvelle"), i.e. the modern business centre, is generally considered to be of highest value both in financial terms and in public opinion. This is especially true for the big urban centers of the Islamic Middle East, while in smaller cities and towns the bazaar and its

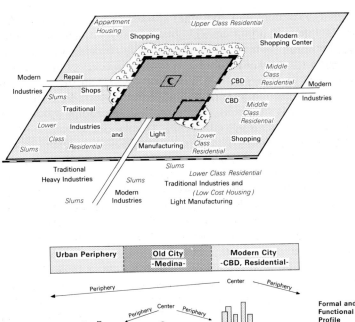

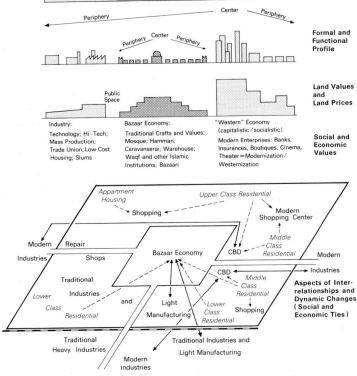

Fig. 3: The Modern Middle Eastern City: A Descriptive Approach

immediate surroundings may still hold the highest land values (cf. Momeni 1976, Rist 1981). Altogether, it may be appropriate to suggest at least a double central-peripheral hierarchy upon the modern city of the Islamic Middle East (fig. 3): that upon the traditional city centre and its bazaar economy is superimposed the present-day city as a whole! It goes without saying that this very general and idealized observation will in reality have to be modified by regional variations according to neighbourhoods, land prices along main arterial roads and other locational factors. Research in this specific field is very rare so far.

Multi-nuclei development and central-peripheral hierarchies within the city of the Islamic Middle East coincide with an often described, never, however, thoroughly investigated, third phenomenon: a deviation and diffusion of traditionally centralized traffic and product flows. In German geography, it was especially Wirth (1974/75) who emphasized the concentration of all economic and social activities in the old city on the one hand, buth who, however, also propagated the idea that urban sprawl and the development of new business districts results in decentralization of supply and demand within the modern city (1968; cf. also Seger 1978). Diffusion of traditionally centralized traffic and money flows coincides with the development of new communication patterns of new and socially segregated areas of preference and/or rejection within the city. Bazaar and madina in this respect stand for low to middle class residential, for traditional crafts, light industries, and traditional bazaar economy with a wide variety of traditional goods and crafts. Ville nouvelle in general and the CBD in special, on the other hand, represent a great variety of residential areas between slums and low cost housing, on the one hand, and luxurious appartment and villa housing, on the other. They stand likewise for modern industries, international banking and travel, for modern retailing and fashionable shopping. For many inhabitants the city falls apart into a number of more or less incoherent and segregated sub-units, with many of which they will never get in touch.

To sum up: The decomposition of the city of the Islamic Middle East into a conglomerate of different nuclei with different forms and functions against the background of a general dualism between old and new is a reality and must be part of any simplifying model (fig. 3). The question, however, remains to what extent such a descriptive model of the city of the Islamic Middle East represents a unique and culture-area-specific phenomenon.

3. The City of the Islamic Middle East: The Functional Aspect and the Problem of City-Hinterland-Relationships

Much has been written, especially in German geography, on the problem of city-hinterland-relationships in the Islamic Middle East. Especially under the influence of Bobek's theory of the rent-capitalistic character of Middle Eastern

urbanism (1959; English version: 1961; 1974, cf. also EHLERS 1978, 1983: WIRTH 1973), quite a few empirical studies have convincingly proven that
- due to a very widespread function of the cities as residence of rural landlords (EHLERS 1977),
- due to urban control and organization of rural demands of almost all kinds of goods and services (BONINE 1980; MOMENI 1976), but also of rural cottage industries (carpet manufacturing; EHLERS 1977, 1982), and
- due to the great social and economic importance of urban based religious institutions

cities in the Islamic Middle East have in the past exerted a tremendous socio-economic pressure and drain on their respective hinterlands. General background of this strangling grip of the cities is the very simple observation that the exchange of goods and services in the Middle East in most cases does not take place in the immediate interrelationship of offer and demand, i.e. between producer and consumer, but only by the mediation of one or several urban based middlemen. The general mechanisms of such inter-urban-exchanges in pre-industrial and rent-capitalistic societies of the Middle East in comparison to those of western industrialized countries are represented in fig. 4. According to BONINE (1980) these mechanism result in a "central place system of dominance"!

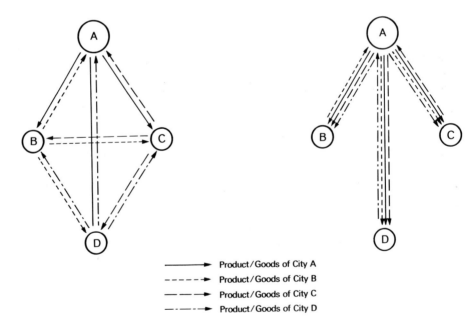

Fig. 4: Model of Inter-Urban Exchange of Goods and Products in a Western Urban Network (left) and in a Pre-Industrial Rent-Capitalistic Urban Network (right)

It is generally accepted that, even more than the hierarchized trading mechanisms of privately offered goods and services, all functions of the public sector, such as government services, public and military administration, and even the clergy, are urban based and localized in a highly hierarchized residential pattern (cf. BILL 1972; SEGER 1975). This means that high ranking functions (universities, hospitals and special clinics, banks, headquarters, and even industries) are first to be found in the capital city, then in provincial centers and only very seldom in inferior centers of regional and/or local importance. In view of the fact that – together with corresponding social hierarchies and disparities – also public services are distributed in the form of a "central place system of dominance", the differences of the settlement networks between industrialized and decentralized countries of the West and those of a central place system of dominance are remarkably obvious (fig. 5): hierarchization of almost all aspects of social and economic activities leads to a hierarchized spatial urban structure in which local and regional administrative units serve as hinterlands for their respective centers, provinces as hinterlands for provincial centers, and the whole country, finally, as hinterland for the national capital (EHLERS 1992).

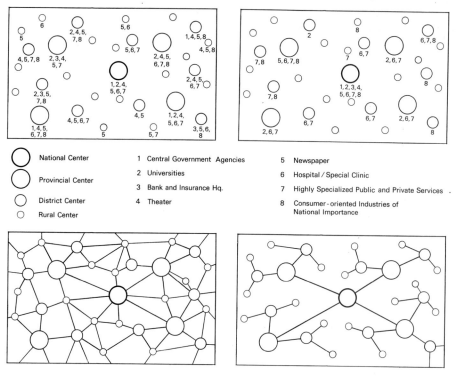

Fig. 5: Central Place System in a Western Urban Network (left) an Central Place System of Dominance in a Pre-Industrial Rent-Capitalistic Urban Network (right)

97

Again, it remains to be questioned if such an urban network and hierarchy is typical for the cities of the Islamic Middle East or if it is to be found also in other Third World or highly centralized countries anywhere else. While there is no doubt that such central place systems of dominance may also occur outside the Islamic Middle East, it is equally doubtless that the analyzed hierarchy and its related city-hinterland-relationships are a very typical, specific and historical phenomenon of the Middle East (EHLERS 1992). BOBEK's arguments in connection with his theory of rent-capitalism, according to which cities already of the ancient Middle East flourished on the basis of their "definitely parasitical character" in regard to their respective hinterlands, are still valid today. Therefore, it is fully justified to consider that the close symbiosis of rent-capitalism and unequal development with its strong and positive repercussions on the cities is a very specific phenomenon of the urbanism of the Islamic Middle East.

Such a central place system of dominance – as idealized in fig. 5 – has very obviously also been observed and described in the very same way already one thousand years ago. According to ISMAIL (1972), the Arab geographer Muqadassi developped theoretical hierarchies of urban centers and attached regions (fig. 6) which resemble very much our own observations and consequences (cf. also SCHOLTEN 1976, esp. pp. 83–117 and fig. 1 and 2).

4. The City of the Islamic Middle East: Spatial and Socio-Economic Consequences of Religious Institutions

Not only in German, but in almost all western geographic discussions about the very essence of the city of the Islamic Middle East, formal and functional aspects of Middle Eastern urbanism have dominated. Islamologists, on the other hand, have from the beginning stressed again and again the overwhelming impact of religious institutions as the decisive and unique feature of the "Islamic city". In this context, they pointed not only to the leading role of the mosque, but – more recently – to the wide variety of "social, political, and legal characteristics" (ABU-LUGHOD 1987) that constitute the "traditional" city in the realm of Islam.

In view of geography's self-defined interest in spatial orders and regional differentiations it is obvious that social, political and/or legal characteristics – including religion and its spatial manifestations – are of geographical relevance as soon as they become a spatial or regional phenomenon. So far geographers, however, have hardly looked at religious manifestations as specific forms of an Islamic urbanity. This is the more surprising since religious institutions such as waqf are of outstanding spatial as well as socio-economic importance for cities and urban life in the Islamic world.

Although the institution of "waqf" (religious endowment) dates back to the very days of the Prophet (BUSSONS DE JANSSENS 1952/53; HEFENING 1934), it is generally accepted that its large scale and city-founding as well as city-forming development started only with the Ottomans and Safavids. Among the great

98

a. Theoretical hierarchy of
   settlements:

1. *Amsār* (sing. *miṣr*), metropolis.

2. *Qaṣabat* (sing. *qaṣabah*),
   fortified provincial capitals.

3. *Mudun* (sing. *madīnah*),
   provincial towns, a main town
   of a district, or a market town.

4. *Qurā* (sing. *qaryah*),
   villages.

b. Theoretical hierarchy of
   regional units:

1. *Aqālīm* (sing. *iqlīm*),
   regions.

2. *Kuwar* (sing. *kūrah*),
   provinces.

3. *Nawāhy* (sing. *nahiyah*),
   districts.

4. *Rustaqāt* (sing. *rustāq*),
   agricultural units.

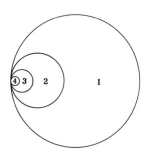

c. Theoretical spatial distribution of settlements:

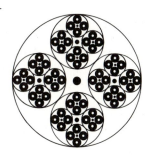

Fig. 6: Muqqadasi's Grading of Settlements and Regional Units and Their Spatial
Distrivution (after ISMAIL)

number of profound and extensive publications by Islamologists and historians of
Islam one may point to the impressive studies of GAUBE on Aleppo (GAUBE-WIRTH
1984, pp. 126–139) and on Esfahan (GAUBE-WIRTH 1978), by INALCIK (1973; 1978;
1990) and MANTRAN (1962) on Istanbul or on those by RAYMOND (1979) on Aleppo
and Cairo. That even nowadays waqf or habous are of great importance has been

99

Geographisches Institut
der Universität Kiel
Neue Universität

shown by Stöber (1986) for Marocco, by Bonine (1987) for Central Iran, or by Khater (1987) for Palestine and Jerusalem.

From a geographical perspective, waqf is of relevance in identifying the uniqueness of the city of the Islamic Middle East in three ways:

– in its spatial impact;
– in its socio-economic importance; and
– in its political aspects.

Waqf – the spatial aspect: Since the Ottomans in 16th century Turkey and the Safavids in 16th–18th century Persia, urban development in the Middle East is almost unthinkable without the institution of waqf. To demonstrate its effects and impacts on urban development it must suffice to quote just one example. 15th and 16th century Istanbul was established around 13 nahiyes, each of which consisted of several neighbourhoods or mahalles (219 altogether) with a mosque, which were supported by waqf of different kinds and size. Table 1 shows mahalles and their waqf endowments for the 13 nahiyes of 16th century Istanbul (Inalcik 1978, p. 229).

Table 1: Waqf Endowments in 13 nahiyes of 16th Century Istanbul (Source: Inalcik 1978)

nahiye	number of mahalles	waqfs in 953/1546	waqfs in 1005/1596
1. Aya Sofya	17	191	345
2. Mahmud Pasha	9	96	115
3. Ali Pasha	5	44	76
4. Ibrahim Pasha	10	106	129
5. Sultan Bayezid	23	198	319
6. Ebu 'l Vefa	12	165	306
7. Sultan Mehemmed	41	372	681
8. Sultan Selim	7	33	90
9. Murad Pasha	23	119	330
10. Davud Pasha	13	84	264
11. Mustafa Pasha	30	65	227
12. Topkapi	7	13	39
13. 'Ali Pasha	22	108	259
Totals:	219	1594	3180

The same source (ibid., p. 231) shows how one has to imagine the construction and management of such a nahiye:

"Davud Pasha Nahiyesi… Kodja Davud Pasha (Grand Vizier from 887/1482 to 902/1497 built a mosque, a hospice, a medrese, a school and a public fountain… with an extensive carshi of 108 shops and 11 ‚rooms' around the mosque. He also brought into occupation the area now named after him on the Marmara coast…, building there a palace, a bath, a bozakhaneh, 11 shops and a landing stage... six baths, in Istanbul and elsewhere, a bedestan at Manastir, shops at Üsküp and Bursa, and the revenues of 12 villages brought in an annual income of 378.886 akce (ca. 7500 ducats)..."

While there is no doubt, that religious endowments in the imperial cities and commercial centers of the Ottoman and Safavid empires received specific attention and promotion, lesser urban centers also greatly benefitted from waqf. A good and probably transferable example is the foundation of the Iranian city of Malayer in 1807 by the Qajar provincial gouvernor: mosque and madrasah were supported by a caravanserai, a timcheh, by 116 shops, by rooms and hamams as well as by the revenues of several villages in the environs of the new city (MOMENI 1976, pp. 29−38). Urban form and function still reflect today the religious waqf-background (fig. 7).

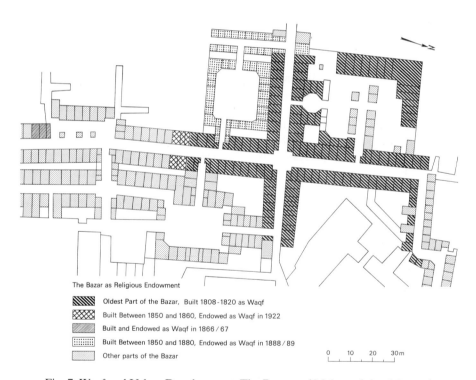

The Bazar as Religious Endowment

▨ Oldest Part of the Bazar, Built 1808-1820 as Waqf

▨ Built Between 1850 and 1860, Endowed as Waqf in 1922

▨ Built and Endowed as Waqf in 1866 / 67

▨ Built Between 1850 and 1880, Endowed as Waqf in 1888 / 89

▨ Other parts of the Bazar

0   10   20   30m

Fig. 7: Waqf and Urban Development: The Bazaar of Malayer (after MOMENI)

Waqf's impact on urban form and function in the cities of the Islamic Middle East is still little known. On the other hand it is very obvious from recent studies by BONINE (1987), EHLERS-MOMENI (1989), KHATER (1987) or STÖBER (1985, 1986) that waqf/habous very obviously has a much bigger share in urban development in the Middle East than has been recognized hitherto.

Waqf – the socio-economic aspect: Besides its importance as a remarkable physical factor in the construction of urban residential and commercial quarters, waqf also plays a considerable socio-economic role in daily life and on specific religious occasions in many cities of the Islamic world. There are, above all, four main functions of waqf in a socio-economic sense:
– provision of a considerable part of religious duties and events for the umma;
– performance of charitable and educational functions such as poor relief, nursing or maintenance of madrasahs and hamams;
– provision of cheap buildings for dwelling, and/or retailing, and/or manufacturing purposes; and
– finally as an employer.

EHLERS-MOMENI (1989) have shown to what extent waqf is able to fulfil a great number of those aforementioned functions still today. The incomes from religious endowments are used for feeding poor people on special occasions, for the maintenance of cisterns, for the provision of light and candles in mosques, or for the performance of religious plays (taziyehs). It is obvious that these functions become apparent especially on religious holidays and in smaller urban centers. Another aspect, which is hardly known so far, is the question of to what extent low rents for waqf-property in the bazaars conribute to the competitiveness of traditional trades and crafts in comparison to modern forms of retail and wholesale trade (cf. BONINE 1987). As to the employment effects, it should be mentioned that waqf employs several hundred peoples, for example, in Morocco alone in its central administration (STÖBER 1986, pp. 101–125), while in Jerusalem the Al-Aqsa Mosque alone has a staff of 157 waqf-employees (KHATER 1987, p. 217), while in the West Banks altogether the waqf-board employs a total of 568 persons (ibid., p. 219).

Waqf – the political aspect: By definition, religious endowments are more or less "eternal" properties of the recipient of the deed and they are unalienable. Even if quite a few waqf endowments in the course of time fell into oblivion and/or many of them changed into private or public hands, others have served their purpose for centuries and continue to do so. In such cases, many endowments in form of mosques, madrasahs, hamams, shops or other properties are more or less persistent structures. It is mainly they that not seldom are physical obstacles to any modernization or change of the urban fabric. The question remains, however, where and to what extent waqf properties really represent obstacles to urban change. This holds true, too, for the aforementioned question of waqf's impact on the persistence and competitiveness of bazaar trades due to low shop rents etc.

The fact that in many countries of the Islamic Middle East, governments have installed specific ministries for waqf-affairs shows the political weigth of this institution still today. STÖBER (1986) has given several examples of cité habous in Morocco, i.e. recent urban quarters constructed on the basis of endowed charities and administered by the „ministère des habous publics et des affaires islamiques".

5. Conclusion:

Academic discussions about the nature of the city in the Islamic world are extensive and controversial. Only recently J. ABU-LUGHOD (1989) asked "What is Islamic about a city?" – again leaving the answer open to future research or to the rejection of the question as such.

The aforementioned considerations in regard to the nature and essence of the city of the Islamic Middle East have shown that very obviously many of the criteria used so far may be far too superficial. This surely holds true for many of the *formal criteria* which – in slightly different shapes and combinations – are typical also for the cities in other cultural areas. Exception is the bazaar which is unique in form, genesis, and function. But what is "Islamic" about it – maybe in parts its origin as a religious endowment?! In regard to *functional terms*, rent-capitalism and a "central place system of dominance" are undoubtedly noteworthy features of the cities of the Islamic Middle East and of its urbanity in general. But again: are there not rent-capitalistic features, exploitive and "parasitical" cities as well as dominant central place systems in other parts of the world? Assuredly there are; but nevertheless rent-capitalism and central place dominance seem to be more pronounced in the Middle East than in other parts of the world. There are reasons for such a statement:
– the area of the present-day Middle East is not only the hub of urban culture, but this urban culture has had a parasitical and exploitive character in regard to its rural hinterlands from the very beginning and over thousands of years;
– ancient Egypt as well as Mesopotamia and other ancient civilizations have been characterized by temple-economies and very often by temple-dominated city states. Even if this tradition may have faded away and occidental urban traditions may have been superimposed on older forms, there is a widespread if not general academic consent that religion is a major component of urbanity in the Islamic Middle East;
– religion, symbolized by the 'djami and its related function, has without doubt greatly contributed to the social, political, and economic supremacy of the cities over their rural hinterlands and to the overall positive image of urban life in comparison to non-urban life styles.

In a recent article, INALCIK (1990) has very strongly argued in favor of an "Islamic city concept", summarizing his findings in the following statement: "…. the waqf system was the key institution in creating a typical Ottoman-Islamic urban structure" (ibid., p. 19). Also from a geographical perspective, the institution of waqf may play a crucial role for a better understanding of the geography of the Middle Eastern city. This is especially true in view of the fact that waqf very obviously functions as just another form of rent-capitalistic channeling of money and goods from rural areas into the cities. Not only the example quoted, but also all other geographical studies published so far point to the fact that whole villages and their agricultural productions were endowed to urban religious institutions and services, thus increasing the rent-capitalistic tendency to concentrate "a good part of the product of agriculture, mining, and other primary branches of production in the cities and put them within reach of a rather broad and differentiated element of the population there, thus giving these cities the possibility of an unheard of rise not only in the number of their inhabitants, but also in material and cultural level" (BOBEK 1961, p. 237). But it were not only these direct benefits to the city and its inhabitants in the form of mosques, hospitals, bazaars, madrasahs or taziyehs. Indirectly they were major urban attractions for the rural populations who had to go to the cities to make use of them. The cities thus at the same time skimmed off whatever small amounts of cash or kind might be available to rural visitors.

Not seldom it has been argued that waqf-like features have been common to medieval European urbanity or to that of other cultural areas as well. This may be basically true, but nevertheless profound differences exist: waqf have always been objects, never subjects – as, for example, in European feudal history! Religious endowments in the Middle East have been the origin and very beginning of quite a few cities – elsewhere too? Djami and waqf are urban centered institutions and it is only the city that benefits from them (JOHANSEN 1981/ 82). And finally: waqf is a modern and persistent institution which still exists and is part of urban form, function, and social life.

Geographers then may have come to an end with their formal and functional approaches in investigating the very nature and essence of what has been called the "Islamic city". Very probably the historian INALCIK is right when he argues: "Anthropologists and geographers will discover ,meaning' only after the necessary ,fieldwork' in the court records of Islamic cities has been done" (1990, p. 21).

The present day city of the Islamic Middle East, however, is more than the historic core of the madina and its specific formal patterns, its functional relationships, and its religious-historic foundations. While these make up its cultural uniqueness, modern developments have contributed to its integration into cosmopolitan urban patterns. As such, any model of the city of the Islamic Middle East has to take into account both its aspects: its traditional core as well as its modern periphery with all the social, economic, and cultural disruptions between these two and within them.

Bibliography:

ABU-LUGHOD, J.: "The Islamic City: Historic Myth, Islamic Essence, and Contemporary Relevance," International Journal of Middle East Studies 19, 1987, pp. 155−176.

Idem, "What is Islamic about a city? Some comparative reflections," Proceedings of the International Conference on Urbanism in Islam, Oct. 22−28, 1989. Tokyo/Japan. Vol 1, pp. 194−217.

BILL, J. A., "The Politics of Iran. Groups, Classes and Modernization," Columbus/Ohio 1972.

BOBEK, H., "Die Hauptstufen der Gesellschafts- und Wirtschaftsentfaltung in geographischer Sicht," Die Erde 90, 1959, pp. 259−298.
Engl. Tr.: "The Main Stages in Socio-Economic Evolution from a Geographical Point of View." Readings in Cultural Geography, ed. P. L. WAGNER and M. W. MIKESELL, Chicago 1961, pp. 218−247.

Idem, "Zum Konzept des Rentenkapitalismus," Tijdschrift voor Economische en Sociale Geografie 65, 1974, pp 73−78.

BONINE, M. E., "Yazd and this Hinterland: A Central Place System of Dominance in the Central Iranian Plateau," Marburger Geogr. Schr. 83, Marburg 1980.

Idem, "Islam and Commerce: Waqf and the Bazaar of Yazd, Iran," Erdkunde 41, 1987, pp. 182−196.

BONINE, M. E. & R. CORDES, "Oil Urbanization. Zum Entwicklungsprozeß eines neuen Typs orientalischer Städte," Geogr. Rundschau 35, 1983, pp. 461−466.

BRUNSCHVIG, R., "Urbanisme médiéval et droit musulman," Revue des Etudes Islamiques 15, 1947, pp. 127−155.

BUSSONS DE JANSSENS, G., "Les Waqf dans l'Islam Contemporain," Revue des Etudes Islamiques, 1951, pp. 1−72, 1953, pp. 43−76.

CORDES, R. & M. E. BONINE, "Abu Dhabi Town. Oil Urbanization in Südostarabien," Geogr. Rundschau 35, 1983, pp. 466−475.

DETTMANN, K., "Islamische und westliche Elemente im heutigen Damaskus," Geogr. Rundschau 21, 1969, pp. 64−68.

Idem, "Städtewesen und Stadtstrukturen im Norden des Industieflandes," Mitt. Fränk. Geogr. Ges. 25/26 (1978/1979), Erlangen 1980, pp. 351−393.

EHLERS, E., "City and Hinterland in Iran: The Example of Tabas/Khorassan," Tijdschrift voor Economische en Sociale Geografie 68, 1977, pp. 284−296.

Idem, "Dezuful und sein Umland," Beiträge zur Geographie orientalischer Städte und Märkte,. ed. G. SCHWEIZER, Beihefte, Tübinger Atlas des Vorderen Orients, Ser. B 24, Wiesbaden 1977, pp. 147−171.

Idem, "Rentenkapitalismus und Stadtentwicklung im islamischen Orient. Beispiel: Iran," Erdkunde 32, 1978, pp. 124−142.

Idem, "Teppichmanufaktur und Teppichhandel in Arak/Faharan-Iran," Der Islam 59, 1982, pp. 222−253.

Idem, "Rent-Capitalism and Unequal Development in the Middle East: The Case of Iran," Work, Income and Inequality. Payment Systems in the Third World, ed. F. STEWART, London 1983, pp. 32−61.

Idem, "Zur baulichen Entwicklung und Differenzierung der marokkanischen Stadt: Rabat − Marrakech − Meknes. Eine Karten- und Luftbildanalyse." Die Erde 115, 1984, pp. 183−208.

Engl.Tr.: "The Structural Development and Differentiation of the Moroccan City: Rabat – Marrakech-Meknes. A Cartographic and Aerial-Photographic Analysis," Applied Geography and Development 28, 1986, pp. 56–83.

Idem, "The City of the Islamic Middle East – a German Geographer's Perspective," Acta Iranica: Textes et Mémoires XVI, Leiden 1990, pp. 68–76.

Idem, "Capitals and Spatial Organization in Iran: Esfahan-Shiraz-Tehran," Téhéran Capitale Bicentenaire, ed. CH. ADLE-B. HOURCADE, Institut Francais de Recherche en Iran, Bibliothêque iranienne vol. 37, Téhéran-Paris 1992, in print.

EHLERS, E. & M. MOMENI, „Religiöse Stiftungen und Stadtentwicklung – Das Beispiel Taft/Zentraliran," Erdkunde 43, 1989, pp. 16–26.

GAUBE, H. & E. WIRTH, „Der Bazar von Isfahan," Beihefte, Tübinger Atlas des Vorderen Orients, Ser. B 22, Wiesbaden 1978.

Idem, „Aleppo. Historische und geographische Beiträge zur baulichen Gestaltung, zur sozialen Organisation und zur wirtschaftlichen Dynamik einer vorderasiatischen Fernhandelsmetropole," Beihefte, Tübinger Atlas des Vorderen Orients, Ser. B 58, Wiesbaden 1984.

GIESE, E., "Transformation of Islamic Cities in Soviet Middle Asia into Socialist Cities," The Socialist City. Spatial Structure and Urban Policy, eds. R. A. FRENCH & F. E. I. HAMILTON, Chichester-New York-Brisbane-Toronto 1979, pp. 145–165.

Idem, „Aufbau, Entwicklung und Genese der islamisch-orientalischen Stadt in Sowjet-Mittelasien," Erdkunde 34, 1980, pp. 46–60.

GRUNEBAUM, G. V., „Die islamische Stadt," Saeculum 6, 1955, pp. 138–153. Engl. Tr.: "The Structure of the Muslim Town," Islam. Essays in the Nature and Growth of a Cultural Tradition, London 1955, pp. 141–158.

HEFFENING, W., "Waqf." Encyclopedia of Islam 4, Leiden 1934, pp. 1096–1103.

INALCIK, H., "The Ottoman Empire. The Classical Age 1300–1600," New York 1973.

Idem, "Istanbul," Encyclopedia of Islam IV, Leiden 1978, pp. 224–248.

Idem, "Istanbul: An Islamic City," Journal of Islamic Studies 1, 1990, pp. 1–23.

ISMAIL, A. A., "Origin, Ideology and Physical Patterns of Arab Urbanization," Ekistics 195, 1972, pp. 113–123.

JOHANSEN, B., "The All-Embracing Town and Its Mosques," Revue de l'Occident Musulman et de la Méditerranée 32, 1981/1982, pp. 139–161.

KARK, R., "The Traditional Middle Eastern City. The Cases of Jerusalem and Jaffa during the Nineteenth Century," Zeitschrift des Dt. Palästina-Vereins, Vol. 97:1, 1981, pp. 94–108.

KHATER, J., "Waqf in der Westbank. Zur wirtschaftlichen, sozialen und politischen Rolle der islamischen religiösen Stiftungen im westlichen Jordanland des ehemaligen Palästinas," Dissertation, Marburg/Lahn 1987.

KOPP, H. & E. WIRTH, „Beiträge zur Stadtgeographie von Sana'a." Beihefte, Tübinger Atlas des Vorderen Orients, Ser. B 95, Wiesbaden 1990.

MANTRAN, R., „Istanbul dans la seconde moitié du XVII siècle. Essai d'histoire institutionelle, économique et sociale," Bibliotheque Archéologique et historique de l'Institut Francais d'Archéologie d'Istanbul 12, Paris 1962.

MARCAIS, G., „La Conception des Villes dans l'Islam". Revue d'Alger 2, 1945, pp. 517–533.

106

Marcais, G., „L'Islamisme et la Vie Urbaine". L'Académie des Inscriptions et Belles Lettres. Comptes Rendus. Paris January-March 1928, pp. 86–100.

Momeni, M., „Malayer und sein Umland. Entwicklung, Struktur und Funktion einer Kleinstadt in Iran," Marburger Geogr. Schr. 68, Marburg 1976.

Raymond, A., „Les grands waqfs et l'organisation de l'espace urbain a Alep et au Caire a l'époque ottomane (XVI–XVII siecles)," Bulletin d'Etudes Orientales de l'Institut Francais de Damas 31, 1979, pp. 113–128.

Rist, B., „Die Stadt Zabol. Zur wirtschaftlichen und sozialen Entwicklung einer Kleinstadt in Ost-Iran (Sistan-Projekt I)," Marburger Geogr. Schr. 86, Marburg 1981.

Scholten, A.: „Länderbeschreibung und Länderkunde im islamischen Kulturraum des 10. Jahrhunderts," Bochumer Geogr. Abhandlungen 25, Paderborn 1976.

Seger, M., „Strukturelemente der Stadt Teheran und das Modell der modernen orientalischen Stadt". Erdkunde 29, 1975, pp. 21–38.

Seger, M., „Teheran, eine stadtgeographische Studie," Wien-New York 1978.

Idem, „Das System der Geschäftsstraßen und die innerstädtische Differenzierung in der orientalischen Stadt (Fallstudie Teheran)," Erdkunde 33, 1979, pp. 113–129.

Smailes, A. E., "The Indian City. A Descriptive Model," Geogr. Zeitschrift 57, 1969, pp. 177–190.

Soffer, A. & Sh. Stern, "The Port City: A Subgroup of the Middle Eastern City Model," Ekistics 316/317, 1986, pp. 102–128.

Stöber, G., "Habous Public in Chaouen. Zur wirtschaftlichen Bedeutung religiöser Stiftungen in Nordmarokko." Die Welt des Islams 25, 1985, pp. 97–125.

Idem, "Habous Public in Marokko. Zur wirtschaftlichen Bedeutung religiöser Stiftungen im 20. Jahrhundert," Marburger Geogr. Schr. 104, Marburg 1986.

Wagstaff, J. M., "The Origin and Evolution of Towns: 4000 BC to 1900 AD," The Changing Middle Eastern City, eds. G. H. Blake & R. J. Lawless, London-New York 1980, pp. 11–33.

Wirth, E., „Strukturwandlungen und Entwicklungstendenzen der orientalischen Stadt," Erdkunde 22, 1968, pp. 101–128.

Idem, „Die Beziehungen der orientalisch-islamischen Stadt zum umgebenden Lande. Ein Beitrag zur Theorie des Rentenkapitalismus," Geographie heute, Einheit und Vielfalt. Ernst Plewe zu seinem 65. Geburtstag, ed. E. Meynen, Wiesbaden 1973, pp. 323–333.

Idem, „Zum Problem des Bazars (suq, carsi). Versuch einer Begriffsbestimmung und Theorie des traditionellen Wirtschaftszentrums der orientalisch-islamischen Stadt," Der Islam 51, 1974, pp. 203–260 and 52, 1975, pp. 6–46.

Idem, „Die orientalische Stadt. Ein Überblick aufgrund jüngerer Forschungen zur materiellen Kultur," Saeculum 26, 1975, pp. 45–94.

Idem, „Dubai. Ein modernes städtisches Handels- und Dienstleistungszentrum am Arabisch-Persischen Golf," Erlanger Geogr. Arbeiten 48, Erlangen 1988.

Wirth, E. (1990): see Kopp, H. & E. Wirth

THE CHINESE CITY

With 12 figures

Wolfgang Taubmann

The fundamental ideas of the Chinese city layout through all dynasties had an unbroken tradition right into the 19th century. The reasons for this continuity might be sought in the stability of the Chinese feudal structure of society as well as in the Confucian ideology and in the significance of the traditional ideas of order.[1]

The history of the Chinese city probably can be traced back to the mythical past of the country, including roughly 3500 years.[2] Obviously, from the very beginning the cities were built according to a fixed plan.

The first and most important hints at the significance of the layout and the size of cities are to be found in the oldest urban construction rules (Zhou li), that probably were issued in the Han period and that describe the ideal capital of the older Zhou dynasty (since the 8th century B. C.).[3]

The Zhou rites set rules for the construction of cities that, though later regionally modified, became of fundamental importance for the urban style during the following 2000 years.[4]

The idealized capital of the Zhou had to be built as a walled square of 9 to 9 li (1 li = 0,5 km) side length, each wall having three gates and orientated to the quarters.[5] Starting from the gates three roads crossed the city, running from north to south and from east to west. In the centre, open to the south, the palace of the emperor had to be situated, to its left in the east the Ancestral Temple and to the right in the west the Altars of Soil and Grain. The market had to be at the back of the palace in the north (fig. 1).

Site, axiality, symmetry, and orientation of the city show different levels of conception, in which Confucian ideology of society as well as cosmological and magical ideas are merged.[6] Therefore Wheatley for instance calls the traditional Chinese city a cosmo-magical symbol.[7] The city reflects the cosmos, the heaven and the square shaped earth. The palace of the emperor is situated in the centre, for as to the hierarchical structure of the Confucian society, the emperor symbolizes the heaven, he is even the Son of Heaven (tianzi).[8] Around the palace in a square or rectangular order from the centre towards the outer walls residential quarters and residential courtyards are to be found. In principle not only a city was walled, but also "every important ensemble of buildings and spaces was a walled enclosure" within the city.[9] Even a courtyard house was a walled ensemble. I.e. the wall was the most essential and permanent element of every city.[10]

Close to the palace the emperor's relatives and his civil and military high ranking officials as well as scholars holding official positions dwelt; people

Model of the Zhou – Dynasty Capital

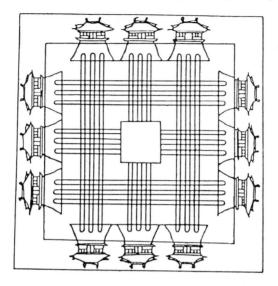

Source : Kaogong Ji of Zhou Li (about 5th century B.C.)

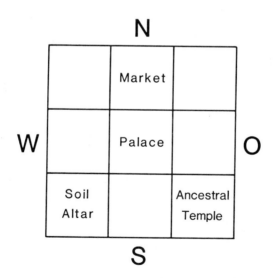

after : Steinhardt 1983, Wu 1986, Ye 1986

Figure 1

belonging to lower classes as artisans and merchants lived further away from the palace.[11] The microcosm is to be found in the microcosm: Just as China is the centre of the earth, the emperor's palace is the centre of the empire. The palace city in the middle had the same layout as the city itself, and even the simple courtyard-house was a microcosm symbolizing a family's structure. Everywhere is to be seen the hierarchical structure of priority and inferiority. Thus the city became the centre of control, even made more easy by a governmentally controlled neighborhood- or ward-system.[12]

The city symbolizing the cosmos, at the same time represents a magic perception of nature. In the geomantic school of feng-shui (wind-water) are to be found the ideas of the dual forces (yin-yang) as well as the closely connected conception of the five elements (wu xing: wood, fire, earth, metal, and water). The site of a city had to be chosen in harmony with nature, i.e. it had to such an extent be part of its surrounding landscape that the "veins of the earth" remained unviolated, and that it gave protection and happiness.[13] Decisions were made in harmony with the movements of the "dragons" and the "waters", i.e. the structure of the mountains and the directions of the rivers and creeks.[14] For instance the site at the south side of a slope was looked upon as favourable, thus detaining the evil spirits from the north.[15]

The four quarters are not only a symbol for the earth, but they also represent the four seasons. Therefore the twelve gates of the ideal city correspond with the twelve months of the year. According to the idea of feng-shui the four quarters were represented by animal signs or elements. The scarlet bird stood for the south or summer, its warmth, sun, and life, whereas the black turtle stood for the north, thus symbolizing winter, coldness, the evil, or the raid of the barbarians. The azure dragon symbolized the east or spring and the white tiger the west or autumn.[16] The south-north axis is the main line of most cities. The south is the seat of yang, i.e. the male, active and light principle; the north is the place of yin, i.e. the female, passive, and dark principle.[17] On the main thoroughfare, going south, the most important buildings are to be found. All these buildings are facing south. The market, located in the north, proves the low rank of trade in the official value-system during the feudal time. Merchants were looked upon as unproductive, just trading goods of other groups. Consequently, the market had to be situated at a place of weakest yang-influence.[18]

The normative conceptions of city building could at their best be realized in the North Chinese Plain or its western spur with the large and flat Wei-valley. Here was the nucleus of Chinese civilization. Rectangular and square city plans are frequent in this area. South of the Changjang there was a broader variety of city plans, as the layout had to adjust to the relief or the net of rivers and channels. However, there exists no concordance between certain city layouts and regional urban systems, as described by SKINNER.[19]

Often only certain elements of the ideal city were realized, as modifications became necessary out of practical reasons. Keeping to the city model was also a

110

question of the position of a city in the administrative hierachy. The imperial capitals or even the provincial capitals as a rule were more carefully planned than e.g. the roughly 2000 towns that were at the very bottom of the administrative hierarchy of the empire. Thus the elements of the ideal city at their best have been realized in the imperial capitals Changan, Loyang, Kaifeng, Nanjing, or Beijing.

In Changan (today Xian) of the Sui- and specially of the Tang-Dynasty (618–906) the main ideas of the above described city model are realized, though modified according to local necessities.[20] Changan itself became the model for the Japanese imperial cities of Nara and Kyoto. The walled city was oriented from north to south, it was rectangular, not square (fig.2). It had three gates in the west, the south, and the east. The main street axis from the palace in the north to the gate of the Scarlet Bird in the south was clearly marked, though in general, Changan had more streets running from north to south (11) and from east to west (14) than is typical for the model city plan. The palace and the city of the emperor were in the north, leaving no room for markets in the north. The site of the then biggest city in the world at the eastern end of the silk road was the basis of widespread trade connections. Thus during the Tang-Dynasty two markets were added, one in the east, the other in the west of the city. Inspite of all variations the "red line" of the model city is quite obvious.[21] Especially the division of Changan into 110 walled wards (fang or li) shows the cellular structure of the city, at the same time pointing out its function as a place of social control.[22] The sections were probably also the basis of neighboring cult communities[23] or guilds, however, they surely were the unities for census or for recruiting soldiers and villeins.[24] In the big cities several fang or li were added to quarters (xiang).[25] At the end of the Tang-Dynasty the walls between the neighborhoods were pulled down, the administrative division of such sections, however, was kept into the Ming-Dynasty.

Xian was already destroyed at the end of the 9th century and became an unimportant administrative centre. At the beginning of the Ming-Dynasty (1368–1644), however, the city was rebuilt, remaining almost unchanged to the end of the 19th century (fig. 3).[26]

The classical city plan is especially well to be seen in Dadu, the forerunner of Beijing.[27] The "Big Capital" of the Mongol ruler Khubilai Khan, founder of the Yuan-Dynasty (1279–1368), was established in 1267. At a site that had an adequate position as well as sufficient water resources,[28] an almost square city with 11 gates was erected, three gates facing west, south and east, however, only two going north. Starting from the gates, streets crossed the city in north-southern and west-eastern direction. The city was divided in 54 quarters (fang), that in themselves were subdivided into four sections by small streets. The fang were inhabited "predominantly by peoples of one occupational, religious, or ethnic group."[29] In the south there were the palace and the city of the emperor, both surrounded by walls. In the east was the Temple of the Ancestors (taimiao), in the

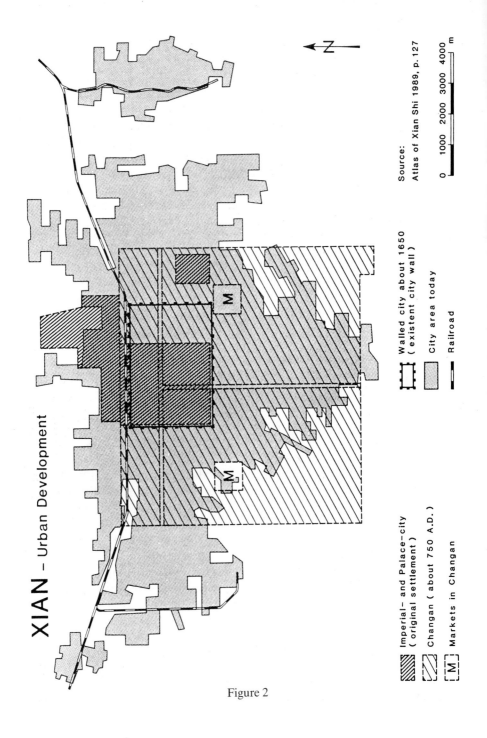

XIAN – Urban Development

Source:
Atlas of Xian Shi 1989, p. 127

Walled city about 1650
(existent city wall)

City area today

Railroad

Imperial- and Palace–city
(original settlement)

Changan (about 750 A.D.)

M Markets in Changan

0 1000 2000 3000 4000
                              m

Figure 2

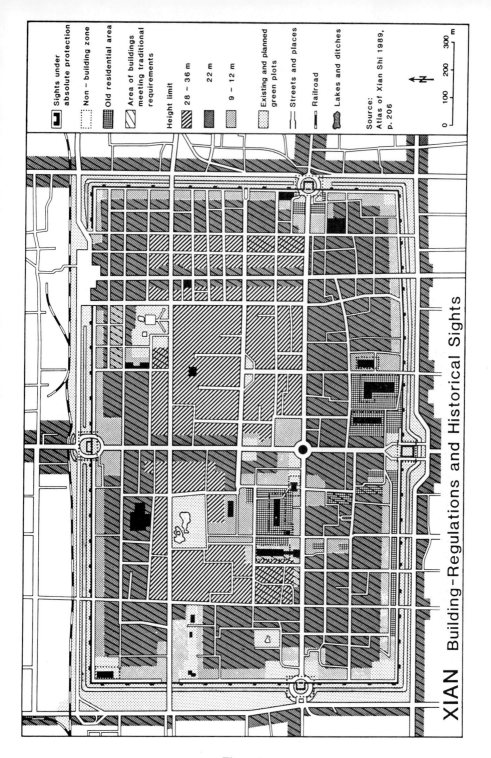

Figure 3

west the Altar of Soil and Grain (shejitan). As laid down in the Zhou rites, the market-place was north of the palace.[30]

Though today nothing much is left of Dadu, the plan of the centre of Beijing in its northern part is laid out in line with the street plan of Dadu. During the Ming-Dynasty the city got its final shape, that remained almost unchanged right into the 20th century. At the beginning of the 15th century (1420) the so-called Inner City (or Tatarian City) as well as the Forbidden City and the Emperor's City were slightly moved south. In the middle of the 16th century (1552) a southern suburb (Outer City, Chinese City) was added. By this change the so-called Tower's Bazaar of Dadu was moved too much to the North. Therefore in the west (Xisi, Xidan), in the east (Dongsi, Dongdan) and the south (Frontcourt Market) of the Forbidden City new markets and shopping streets were established, that are still in use. Especially in the south, in the so-called Outer City, a vivid quarter for merchants, craftsmen, and entertainers was established.[31]

The Temple of the Ancestors (today the cultural palace of the working-class) and the Temple of Soil and Grain (today Zhongshan Park) were moved to the southside of the Forbidden City. The main north-south axis of almost 8 km length now ran from the Bell Tower and Drum Tower, erected in the centre of former Dadu, to the top of the Coal Hill, the Main Halls of the Forbidden City and the Zhengyangmen, that separated the Inner and Outer city, and continued right to the south gate of the Outer City.[32]

The importance of this huge axis was further accentuated in the south by the Temple of Heaven (tiantan) at its eastern and the Altar of Agriculture (xiannongtan) at its western side (fig. 4). There was a great number of other temples: In the north of the capital was the Temple of the Earth (ditan) balancing the Temple of Heaven. As the earth symbolizes the yin-principle in contrast to the yang-principle of the Tiantan, this temple had to be in the north. In the east (growth, spring) was the Temple of Sun (ritan), in the West the Altar of Moon (yuetan).[33]

Fundamental elements of the classical city model, though not so strictly realized, are also to be found in the city plan of Pingjiang (today Suzhou), a regional centre of the Southern Song-Dynasty.[34] Wall as well as streetplan are of rectangular shape, typical, too, for the channel system. The city was crossed by three streets, running from east to west, and four going from north to south. The prefecture's seat lay in the south of the city. Instead of twelve gates there were only six, one of them the Water Gate (shui men) in the southeast. Such water gates were frequent in regions, where the traffic used waterways.

Another example of a modified city plan is Chengdu, situated in an irrigated alluvial plain in Sichuan, with a history "traceable to the Spring and Autumn period (770−475 B. C.)".[35] At the beginning of the Yuan-Dynasty the city was destroyed and later reconstructed as the seat of an imperial prince. Even by a destruction at the beginning of the 17th century the original city plan remained unchanged (fig. 5).[36] The nucleus of the settlement, i.e. the palace of the Ming

114

BEIJING   Building–Regulations and Historical Sites

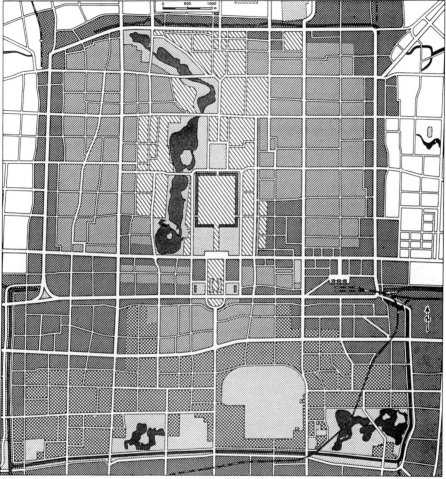

Height limit

- ▓ No limit
- ▒ Max. 6 floors (up to 18 m)
- ▨ Max. 4 floors (up to 12 m)
- ▧ Max. 3 floors (up to 9 m)

- ▤ Green plots / parks
- ◆ Lakes, creeks etc.
- ▬ Railroad
- ⇌ Streets

Source: Beijing Municipal Institute of City Planning and Design

Figure 4

Plan of CHENGDU about 1700 A.D. (Qing – Dynasty)

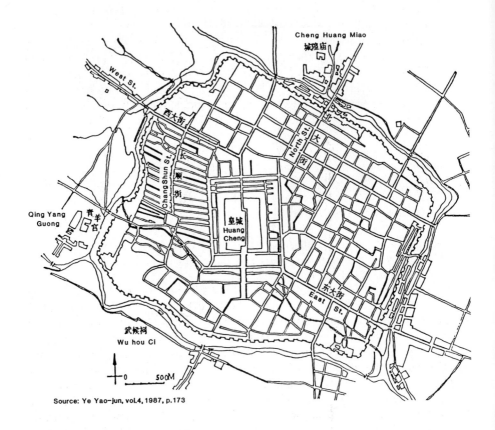

Source: Ye Yao-jun, vol.4, 1987, p.173

Figure 5

prince, once surrounded by walls, looks from north to south, whereas the city itself, surrounded by a wall with four gates, is oriented from north-east to south-west and from north-west to south-east. The streets were laid out according to a chequered plan, the only straight road of some lenght was the so-called East-Street, running from the East Gate to the south-eastern corner of the palace. An explanation for this deviation from north-south might be found in the fact, that the city walls were built along the rivers, thus using the waterways as natural moats. Just as in other cities (Tatarian City in Beijing, Xian) the Manchu of the Quing-Dynasty, after having conquered China, separated themselves from the local people by living in a city quarter of their own. Even today the Manchu city is to be recognized in a section of Chengdu, where the streets run as if forming a ladder.

About 1920 roughly 0.6 million inhabitants were mainly living inside the walls. Chengdu, away from the centre of China, had many pre-modern traits, such as unpaved streets and sewage running in open ditches.

Chengdu and Suzhou already show many modifications of the ideal city model. These were, however, more frequent in the almost 2000 towns, at the bottom of the administrative hierarchy. Almost all towns had a wall just as the prefecture cities and the capitals of the provinces, since the wall was the essential component of a city.[37] However, the majority of the towns had only four gates. There is a limited number of temples, markets, examination halls and the like, being the special attributes of big cities. The Yamen was the seat of the imperial administrator, who was the keeper of the seal. There was a Confucian temple, a temple of the City God, and a Buddhist temple. In some streets and public places there were shops and smaller periodic markets. Freqently close to the walls a larger area was used for gardening, because the city wall was planned more extensive than actually necessary for the settlement.[38] The latter holds also true for bigger cities.

There are many examples for the type of the imperial county city (see fig. 6). A small city in the province of Sichuan, mapped by Prof. Lin Chao in the middle of the 1930s, still shows all characteristic features (fig. 7).[39]

A good example for the type of a county seat is also the Shanghai of the 17th century, having got that function during the Yuan-Dynasty.[40] Only in the middle of the 16th century Shanghai got an oval bricked wall of 5 km length and 7 m height with six street gates and four water gates, protecting the town against Japanese piratry, that became more and more frequent. Two parks and one temple showed that the then 100,000 inhabitants were rather well off.

The area of walled Shanghai was about 2 km², its extension being comparable to that of many smaller cities. However, in comparison to the walled area of Beijing with 63 km², Suzhou with 14.8 km², Xian with 12 km², or Chengdu with 11.5 km², Shanghai was rather small.[41]

Shanghai, the city above the sea, is not only an example of a wealthy county city, but also of the decisive change the traditional Chinese cities had to undergo in the middle of the 19th century, when foreign businessmen and their capital invaded the coastal regions and the lower courses of the rivers. The semi-colonial status under foreign predominance also meant the end of traditional social structures and a fundamental change of the old Chinese city (fig. 8). In the central and western parts of the country with an underdevelopped traffic system, however, traditional city conceptions could survive, as to be seen e.g. in Chengdu.

In cities such as Shanghai, Tianjin, Dalian, Qingdao, Amoy (today Xiamen), Ningbo, Guangzhou, or even Wuhan modern industrial plants were erected as well as European residences in the concession areas, banks, shopping centres, or hotels, that look like a collection of the then modern European and North American buildings.

Typical Plan of an Imperial County City

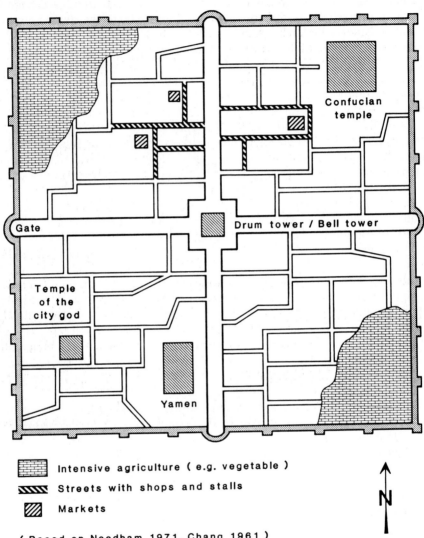

Confucian temple

Gate

Drum tower / Bell tower

Temple of the city god

Yamen

▨ Intensive agriculture (e.g. vegetable)

〰 Streets with shops and stalls

▨ Markets

(Based on Needham 1971, Chang 1961)

N

Figure 6

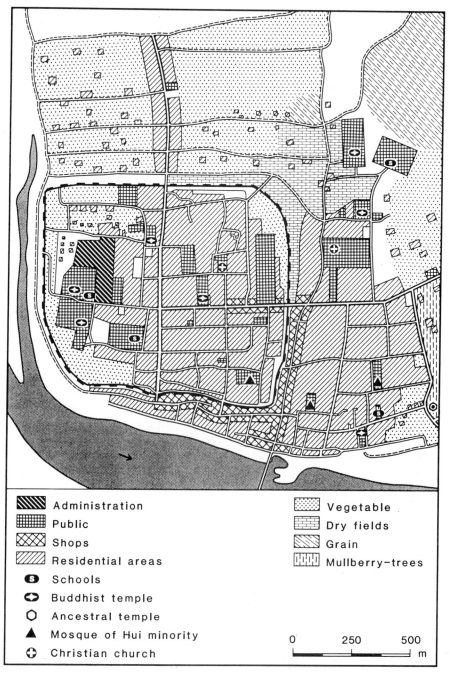

Administration		Vegetable	
Public		Dry fields	
Shops		Grain	
Residential areas		Mullberry-trees	
S	Schools		
Buddhist temple			
Ancestral temple			
▲	Mosque of Hui minority		
Christian church		0 250 500 m	

Based on an unpublished map drawn by Prof. Lin Chao, about 1935

Figure 7: A Typical Small City in Sichuan Province in the 1930s

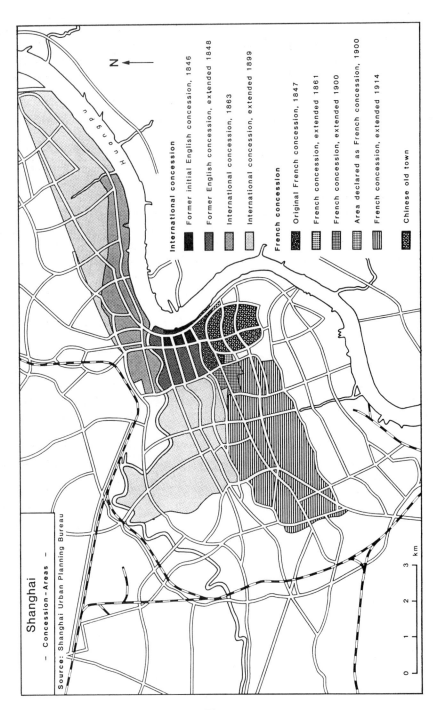

Figure 8

Characteristic traits of traditional Chinese cities were the walls, protecting them against the outside world and allowing controls in the inside, as well as a palace or ceremonial buildings, ministries, offices, libraries, schools, archives, warehouses, markets, inns, and shops. In short, the city was the centre of authority, administration, and scholarship, but at the same time also of consumption and suppression. The cities supported a feudal society. There was no chance for a democratic citizenship, the common people had neither legal security nor civic rights.

The partly radical alterations of the cities in the People's Republic of China were dictated by urgent necessities, long-suppressed hate as well as by ideological ideas. On the other hand, during the last years there is also to be seen a continuity of traditional elements, though partly changed. There were fundamental economic and political concepts for city development, such as a levelling of areal socio-economic differences, reasonable land use, or the development of a cellular structure as an expression of the concept of neighborhoods and a local coordination of living, working, and supply. The transformation of the ancient cities, however is better described in the categories of concentration and growing variety of land use, demolition and construction, or the deliberate transformation of city-elements that stood for feudal architecture. Especially the city walls were pulled down already in the fifties or sixties. In some cities the destruction of the walls started already at the end of the empire, e.g. in Shanghai in 1911/12.

It was the parasitic character of the cities that provided the background for urban policy at the very start. By the slogan "Change the cities of consumption into cities of production!" the wave of industrialization was started, often without taking into consideration traditional structures. The growth of the population in the centres of the cities and the increasing number of plants as well as a housing concentration was typical for the first decades after the foundation of the PRC.[42]

First of all more and more people moved into the traditional residential areas. Though already before 1949 several families lived in the courtyard-houses in northern Chinese cities, because only very rich families had the means of living in one by themeselves, today between seven to nine families, i.e. 25 to 30 persons, are sharing a courtyard-house. An example of such a home on the northern part of the old city of Beijing demonstrates quite clearly this process of concentration (fig. 9): In the early fifties its layout could clearly be recognized, in 1987, however, the built-up area had grown by about 55 %, thus leading to an inner concentration. As a rule the process of concentration leads to constructions of low quality. Thus, not taking into consideration some exceptions, the traditional courtyard-house today is regarded as a transitional phenomenon that sooner or later will have disappeared.[43] The renewal of whole sections of old cities in many cases implies the destruction of a unique architecture. Economic efficiency and quickness are the reasons for an industrialized way of building with pre-fabricated elements, often ending up in an urban landscape of great monotony.

This monotony of residential areas becomes even more obvious, because

Built-up Courtyard House in BEIJING

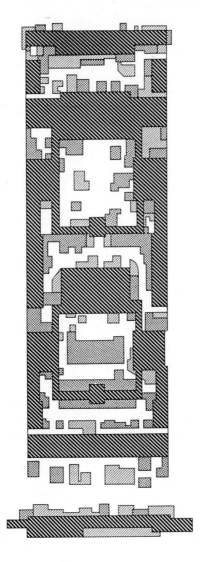

▨▨ – built-on area in the early 1950s

▨▨ – additional buildings from beginning of 1950s to the end of 1970s

▨▨ – additional buildings from the end of 1970s up to 1987

Source: Wu Liang-Yong 1989

Figure 9

usually it is to be found in combination with further elements of the so-called socialist city planning: large streets or crossings – often planned by Soviet city planners – extended places, parks, and sports fields.

In no other Chinese city was the centre more strictly remodelled according to socialist ideology than in Beijing. This can be demonstrated by the transformation of the Tiananmen Square.[44] South of the Gate of Heavenly Peace (Tiananmen) since the Ming-Dynasty there was a T-shaped palace-place, surrounded by red brick walls, the "Corridor of the Thousand Steps". At both sides of this place were to be found central offices, ministries, and the five headquarters of the imperial army. This corridor being part of the segmented north-south axis, was meant for those who approached the palace from the southside to be able to admire the Tiananmen Gate from a specially impressive angle.

Immediately after the end of the Qing-Dynasty the place was opened to traffic and "became the political focus of the republic".[45] In 1959 in honour of the 10th anniversary of the PRC the red walls were completely pulled down. The Tiananmen as the new centre of Beijing as well as the heart of all China, was laid out as such a huge open square that even the emperor's palace was supposed to look like its "backyard". The same holds true for the new west-east axis, built at the same time as the extension of the Tiananmen. This Changan-Street, the new counteraxis of 120 m width, was to eliminate the predominance of the traditional feudal north-south axis. The new monumental buildings east and west of the Tiananmen Square were to represent the new centre of political activities (Great Hall of the People) as well as to express the modern way of interpreting history (Museum of Chinese History and Revolution). On the north-south axis the "Mao Zedong Memorial Hall" was erected in 1977, showing some traits of classical imperial architecture (double roof, basement). The entrance gate of the mausoleum facing north, means a definite break with tradition, for in feudal times the entrances of palaces and public buildings were always looking south. The sarcophagus of Mao, too, lies in a north-south axis, the corpse itself facing north, in contrast to the ancient emperors looking south. Mao "looks" down and back on the olden times of the empire.

In many cities are to be found less spectacular examples of remodelling the centres. In Chengdu, for instance, the dilapidating palace-city in the centre was pulled down and replaced by an exhibition hall and a Mao statue.

In the last few years, however, in some cities the reappraisal of historical heritage can be observed.[46] After the demolition of the centre of Beijing was already far advanced, a more restrictive plan for the old core is now to regulate the height of the buildings near the imperial palace, in the emperor's city and in the still existent old residential streets (fig. 4). In Xian since 1983 the almost 14 km long wall and the moat from the time of the Ming-Dynasty have been restored and surrounded by a green belt. Historical buildings and some parts of Xian's urban core are nowadays under protection or under restrictive building regulations (fig. 3).[47]

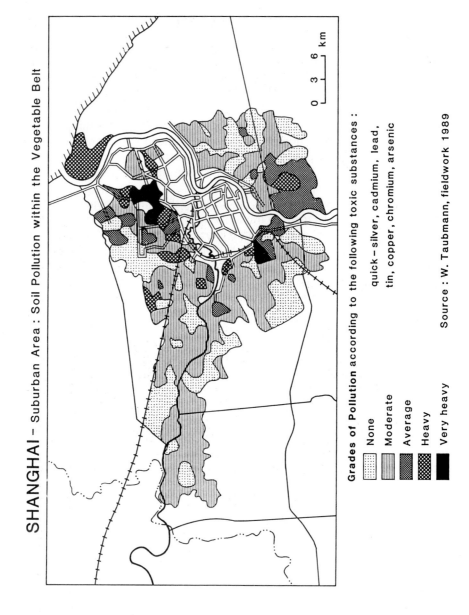

SHANGHAI – Suburban Area : Soil Pollution within the Vegetable Belt

Grades of Pollution according to the following toxic substances :

quick – silver, cadmium, lead,
tin, copper, chromium, arsenic

None
Moderate
Average
Heavy
Very heavy

Source : W. Taubmann, fieldwork 1989

Figure 10

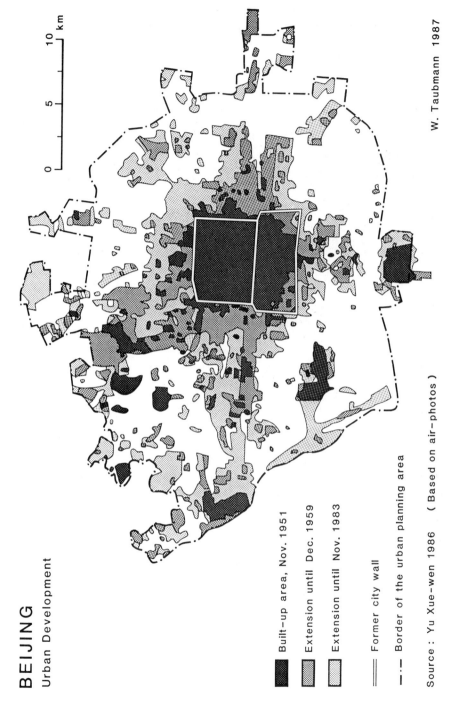

BEIJING
Urban Development

10 km

W. Taubmann 1987

■ Built-up area, Nov. 1951

▨ Extension until Dec. 1959

▨ Extension until Nov. 1983

‖ Former city wall

–··– Border of the urban planning area

Source: Yu Xue-wen 1986   (Based on air-photos)

Figure 11

A Model of Chinese City
– Form and Landuse –

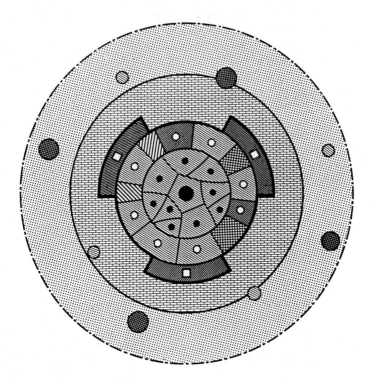

● Old core

● Old service and shopping centre

○ New service and shopping centre (up to ca. 1980)

□ New service and shopping centre (after ca. 1980)

  Industrial / residential unit (streetbureau, inhabitants' committee

  Industry

  Administration, cultural institutions

  Residential units

  Satellite towns

  Towns and townships

  Vegetable cultivation

  Grain and industrial crops

—.— Administrative boundary

W. Taubmann, based on Lo, 1979

Figure 12

The overcrowding of the inner cities already at the end of the 50s is responsible for the construction of new buildings in empty and cleared inner-urban spaces as well as for the erection of so-called new villages for workers, often in the neighborhood of recently established plants.

As there is a constant and urgent need of flats in big cities, large housing estates have been established at the outskirts of these cities, specially since the beginning of the economic reform at the end of the 70s. Even today there is an on-going discussion on relieving the city core by erecting satellite towns. Several of these have already been realized, e.g. in the case of Shanghai or Beijing.

This discussion has to be seen against the background of severe land use conflicts, caused by the competition between agricultural use of the surrounding countryside and the growing urban and industrial demands on the same area. In general the agricultural area is not only permanently reduced, but also heavily polluted (fig. 10). As the cities grow less along traffic axes but more in circles round the centre (fig. 11) and as their inner social differentiation is not conspicuous, form and use of a modern Chinese city can best be described in a concentric model (fig. 12).[48]

The inner areas round the old core are of mixed use combining living and working. They are subdivided into sections by the system of street-offices or inhabitants' committes, often having their own supply and service centre. In the outer zone extended monofunctional units (e.g. cultural institutions, industrial units) are increasing in number. The most recent extension is dominated by big housing estates. The garden zone shows that most cities have their own vegetable supply. The compact form of the cities is caused by the rather limited capacity of the transport system, forcing even the vegetable zone to be as close as possible to the city's centre. Only at the outer rim or beyond the garden zone are satellite towns to be found. The old city centres are under the permanent pressure of transformation, thus losing more and more of their local architectural tradition and individuality.

References

Atlas of Xian Shi (Chinese). Xiang: Atlas Publishing House 1989.

BOYD, A.: Chinese Architecture and Town Planning 1500 B. C. – A. D. 1911. London: Alec Tiranti 1962.

CHANG SEN-DOU: The Chinese Hsien Capital: A Study in Historical Urban Geography. Ph. D. thesis. Washington: University of Washington 1961.

CHANG SEN-DOU: Some Observations on the Morphology of Chinese Walled Cities. In: Annals of the AAG, vol., 60, 1970, pp. 63−91.

CHANG SEN-DOU: The Morphology of Walled Capitals. In: SKINNER, W. (ed.): The City in Late Imperial China. Stanford: University Press 1977, pp. 75−100.

DE GROOT, J. J. M.: Universalismus, die Grundlagen der Religion, Ethik, des Staatswesens und der Wissenschaften Chinas, Berlin 1919.

DIETSCH, K. A.: Staat und Gesellschaft. In: GOEPPER, R.: Das alte China. Geschichte und Kultur des Reiches der Mitte. München: Bertelsmann 1988, pp. 113–148.

DWYER, D. J.: Chengdu, Sichuan: the Modernization of a Chinese City: In: Geography, vol. 71, 1986, pp. 215–227.

EBERHARD, W.: Structure of the Chinese City in the Pre-Industrial Period. In: Economic Development and Cultural Change, Vol. 4, 1955/56, pp. 253–268.

Fakultät Architektur der Qinghua-Universität: Die antike Architektur Chinas. Beijing: Verlag der Qinghua-Universität 1985.

GOEPPER, R.: Das alte China. Geschichte und Kultur des Reiches der Mitte. München: Bertelsmann 1988.

GRANET, M.: Die chinesische Zivilisation. München: Deutscher Taschenbuch Verlag 1980.

HAN JI: Planning Thought of Liang Sicheng and Protection of Ancient City of Xi'an. Paper presented at the Beijing International Symposium on Historic Cities and Modernization, 12–16 May, 1989, Beijing.

HOA, LÉON: Reconstruire la Chine – trente ans d'urbanisme 1949–1979. Paris: Editions du Moniteur 1981.

HOFMEISTER, B.: Die Stadtstruktur. Darmstadt. Wiss. Buchges. 1980 (Beiträge der Forschung, vol. 132).

HOU REN-ZHI: On Theory and Practice in Historical Geography (Chinese). Shanghai 1979.

HOU REN-ZHI: Historical Atlas of Beijing (Chinese). Beijing: Historical Atlas Committee 1985.

HOU REN-ZHI: The Transformation of the Old City of Beijing, China. In: CONZON, M. P.: (ed.): World Patterns in Modern Urban Change. Essays in Honor of Chauncy D. Harris. Chicago: Department of Geography 1986, pp. 217–239.

LIU LAURENCE G.: Chinese Architecture. London: Academy Editions 1989.

LO, C. P.: Spatial Forms and Land Use Patterns of Modern Chinese Cities: An Exploratory Model: In: LEE, NGOK and LEUNG CHI-KEUNG (eds.): China: Development and Challenge, Vol. 2: Political Economy and Spatial Pattern and Process. Hong Kong: Centre of Asian Studies, University of Hong Kong 1979, pp. 233–258.

MATZAT, W.: Jiaozhou, Provinz Shandong: Entwicklung einer chinesischen Kleinstadt im 20. Jahrhundert. In: FÜLDNER, E. (ed.): Stadtgeographische Aspekte – Studien zur regionalen Stadtgeographie und ihrer Didaktik. Festschrift für Siegfried Gerlach zum 60. Geburtstag. Ludwigsburg 1990, pp. 179–193.

NEEDHAM, J.: Science and Civilisation in China, Vol. IV, Part III, Cambridge: The University Press 1971, pp. 71–79.

P'ENG TSO-CHIH: Chinesischer Städtebau unter besonderer Berücksichtigung der Stadt Peking. In: Nachrichten der Gesellschaft für Natur- und Völkerkunde Ostasiens/ Hamburg, vol. 89/90, June 1961, pp. 5–80.

PANNELL, C. W.: Past and Present City Structure in China. In: The Town Planning Review, vol. 48, 1977, pp. 157–172.

PEISERT, CHR.: Der Tiananmen-Platz – Überlegungen zum Wandel der symbolischen Funktionen eines Zentrums. Mimeo, no year. 19 pp.

PEISERT, CHR.: Platz des Himmlischen Friedens. Architektur und Politik im Zentrum Pekings. in: H. STECKEL (ed.): China im Widerspruch. Hamburg: Rowohlt 1988, pp. 183–201.

PIRAZZOLI-T'SERSTEVENS, M.: China. Fribourg: Office de Livre 1970. (Architektur der Welt).

128

REICHERT, F.: „Heimat der Ballen und Fässer". Grundzüge einer Stadtgeschichte. In: ENGLERT, S./F. REICHER (eds.): Shanghai: Stadt über dem Meer. Heidelberg: Heidelberger Verlagsanstalt und Druckerei 1985, pp. 41–89 (= Heidelberger Bibliotheksschriften, 17).

ROWE, W. T.: Hankow. Commerce and Society in a Chinese City, 1796–1889. Stanford: Stanford University Press 1984.

SCHINZ, A.: Die Entwicklung der Stadt Xian, Provinz Shaanxi/China, seit den Reisen Ferdinand von Richthofens. In: Die Erde, vol. 114, 1983, pp. 147–164.

SIRÉN, O.: The Walls and Gates of Peking. London: John Lane 1924.

SKINNER, W.: (ed.): The City in Late Imperial China. Stanford: University Press 1977.

STEINHARDT, N. S.: The Plan of Khubilai Khan's Imperial City. In: Artibus Asiae, vol. 44, 1983, pp. 137–158.

STEINHARDT, N. S.: Chinese Imperial City Planning. Honolulu: University of Hawaii Press 1990.

TAYLOR, R.: Chinese Hierarchy in Comparative Perspective. In: The Journal of Asian Studies 48, no. 3, 1989, pp. 490–511.

THILO, TH. Klassische chinesische Baukunst. Wien: Editon Tusch 1977.

VON MENDE, E.: Wirtschaft. In: GOEPPER, R.: Das alte China. Geschichte und Kultur des Reiches der Mitte. München: Bertelsmann 1988, pp. 149–186.

WALLACKER, B. E. et al. (eds): Chinese Walled Cities: A Collection of Maps from Jokaku no Gaiyo. Hong Kong: The Chinese University Press 1970.

WHEATLEY, P.: The Pivot of the Four Quarters: Edinburgh: University Press 1971.

WRIGHT, A. F.: The Cosmology of the Chinese City: In: SKINNER, W. (ed.): The City in Late Imperial China. Stanford: University Press 1977, pp. 33–73.

WU LIANGYONG: A Brief History of Ancient Chinese City Planning. Kassel: Gesamthochschulbibliothek 1986 (= Urbs et regio, Sonderband 38).

WU LIANGYONG: After a New Prototype: Rehabilitation of Residential Areas in the Old City of Beijing. Paper presented at the Beijing International Symposium on Historic Cities and Modernization, 12–16 May, 1989, Beijing.

WU, N. I.: Architektur der Chinesen und Inder. Ravensburg: Otto Maier 1963 (= Große Zeiten und Werke der Architektur – vol. 9).

YANG WU-YANG: The Context of Beijing's Commercial Network – An Emperical Study on the Central Place Model. In: Geo Journal, vol. 21, nos. 1/2, 1990, pp. 49–55.

YE XIAOJUN: Atlas of Historical Capitals of China (Chinese). 4 vols., Lanzhou: Lanzhou University Publishing House 1986/87.

YU QINGKANG: Chinese Cultural Heritage and Modern Urban Development. In: China City Planning Review, vol. 6, no. 1, 1990, pp. 3–9.

ZHENG XIAOXIE: The "Red Line" Underlying the Planning of Capital Layout in Ancient China. In: China City Planning Review, vol. 1, no. 1, 1985, pp. 28–48.

Notes:

1) Comp. LIU 1988 or WRIGHT 1977.
2) Comp. eg. DIETSCH 1988, pp. 122f.
3 The Kao gong ji ("Record of Artificer/Trade"), a section of the Zhou Li ("Zhou's Book of Rites), is supposed to be added to the Zhou li in the "late first milemnium B.

C. "(Steinhardt 1990, p. 33). According to Wu (1986, p. 3) "written in the early period of the Warring States." See also Thilo 1977, pp. 171f. or Wheatley 1971, p. 411.

4) Comp. eg. Liu 1988, p. 20f.

5) Pirazolli-t'Serstevens, M./Bouvier, N. 1970, p. 10.

6) The conception of universalism used by de Groot may perhaps be regarded as a general term for all schools (de Groot 1918).

7) Wheatley 1971, p. 411.

8) Comp. eg. B. Liu 1988, p. 20f.

9) Boyd 1962, p. 49.

10) P'eng 1961, p. 26.

11) Taylor 1989, pp. 490f.

12) Steinhard 1990, p. 9.

13) See also Granet 1980, p. 102f.

14) P'eng, p. 10.

15) Comp. eg. Thilo 1977.

16) Steinhardt 1990, p. 8.

17) Thilo 1977, pp. 17f.

18) Wright 1977, p. 49.

19) Skinner 1977, p. 217.

20) Comp. eg. Wu 1963, p. 36/37.

21) Comp. Zheng 1985, pp. 28 ff.

22) von Mende 1988, p. 181.

23) Hofmeister 1980, p. 96; Steinhardt 1990, p. 9.

24) Pirazolli-t'Serstevens, M./Bouvier, N. 1970, p. 40.

25) Eberhard 1955/56, p. 261.

26) Compare the detailed description by Schinz 1988, pp. 147ff.

27) Detailed version by Steinhardt 1983, pp. 137f.

28) Thilo 1977, p. 179.

29) Steinhardt 1990, p. 9/10.

30) Wu Liangyong 1986, pp. 50f.

31) Yang 1990, p. 50.

32) Hou 1986, pp. 228f.

33) Thilo 1977, pp. 200f.

34) Boyd 1962, pp. 54f.

35) Steinhardt 1990, p. 24; see also Dwyer 1986, pp. 15f.

36) Schinz 1989, pp. 272f.

37) The term cheng means wall as well as city. See also Chang 1977, pp. 75f. According to Steinhardt 1990, p. 27: "Cheng is the most common second syllable in the name of a walled city..."

38) Detailed description of country cities by Chang 1961.

39) The late Prof. Lin Chao, Peking University, kindly gave me the unpublished map.

40) Comp. Reichert 1985, pp. 41f.

41) Chang 1977, Tab. 2 and 3.

42) This process is described in detail for the small town Jiaozhou/Shandong by Matzat 1990.

43) See also Hoa 1981, pp. 170ff.
44) Comp. Hou 1979 and 1986; Peisert (no year is given) and Peisert 1988; Steinhardt 1990, pp. 179f.
45) Steinhardt 1990, pp. 179f.: May Forth Movement 1919, May Thirthieth Movement 1925, December Ninth Movement 1935, proclamation of the PRC on October First 1949.
46) Comp. eg. Yu 1990.
47) Han 1989, p. 9.
48) Comp. also Lo 1979, pp. 253f.

Anschriften der Autoren

Prof. Dr. Jürgen Bähr
Geographisches Institut der Universität Kiel, Ludewig-Meyn-Str. 14, D-2300 Kiel

Prof. Dr. Eckart Ehlers
Geographische Institute der Universität Bonn, Meckenheimer Allee 166, D-5300 Bonn 1

Prof. Chauncy D. Harris, Ph. D., D.Litt.,Drs.h.c.
Dept. of Geography, University of Chicago, 5828 University Ave., Chicago, Illinois 60637, U.S.A.

Prof.Dr. Burkhard Hofmeister
Institut für Geographie der Technischen Universität Berlin, Budapester Str. 44−46, D-1000 Berlin 30

Prof. Dr. Elisabeth Lichtenberger
Institut für Geographie der Universität Wien, Universitätsstr. 7, A-1010 Wien, Österreich

Prof. Dr. Walter Manshard
Institut für Kulturgeographie der Universität Freiburg, Werderring 4, D-7800 Freiburg i.Br.

Prof. Dr. Günter Mertins
Geographisches Institut der Universität Marburg, Deutschhausstr. 10, D-3550 Marburg/Lahn

Prof. Dr. Wolfgang Taubmann
Studiengang Geographie, FB 8 der Universität Bremen, Bibliotheksstr., D-2800 Bremen 33

Prof. Dr. Herbert Wilhelmy
Geographisches Institut der Universität Tübingen, Hölderlinstr. 12, D-7400 Tübingen